DANCING WITH THE FAMILY

A
Symbolic-Experiential
Approach

DANCING WITH THE FAMILY

A
Symbolic-Experiential
Approach

By

Carl A. Whitaker, M.D.

and

William M. Bumberry, Ph.D.

BRUNNER/MAZEL *Publishers* • NEW YORK

Library of Congress Cataloging-in-Publication Data

Whitaker, Carl A.
  Dancing with the family: A symbolic-experiential approach / by
Carl A. Whitaker and William M. Bumberry.
    p.   cm.
    Accompanied by a videotape.
    Bibliography: p.
    ISBN 0-87630-496-X
    1. Family psychotherapy — Case studies. 2. Experiential
psychotherapy — Case studies.   I. Bumberry, William M.
II. Title.
    [DNLM: 1. Family Therapy methods.   WM 430.5.F2 W577d]
    RC488.5.W48   1988   616.89'156 — dc19   87-36843
    DNLM/DLC   CIP
    for Library of Congress

Published by
BRUNNER/MAZEL, INC.
19 Union Square
New York, New York 10003

MANUFACTURED IN THE UNITED STATES OF AMERICA

10 9 8 7 6 5 4 3 2

CONTENTS

PREFACE

At 8:00 o'clock, on a Monday morning, late in the summer of 1981, I was seated outside Carl Whitaker's office, awaiting his arrival. This was to be my initial encounter with Carl, a blind date of sorts. Three years out of graduate school, I viewed this as an opportunity for an exciting learning experience. With resumé in hand, I waited nervously. The time was spent preparing a witty opening line and a thank-you for having accepted my request for a three-day visit.

A few moments later he rounded the corner. As I rose to greet him, a mother . . . then, a father . . . then, three children followed him to his office door. Something was wrong! This was not what I had planned! Before I could process what was happening, Carl said, "Hi, you must be Bill. Come on in and we'll get started." Dazed, I trailed the family into Carl's office, somehow managed to be seated, then promptly melted into the couch. True, I had come to learn about symbolic-experiential therapy, but I hadn't anticipated being the patient!

By the time noon arrived, four families had been seen. As the morning passed, I had recovered from my stupor, emerged from the initial sense of unreality, and begun to enjoy the experience. The afternoon brought two additional families, a couple, and a supervisory session with one of the residents.

At 5:30, following the last family session, I was exhausted! The day had been filled with tension, excitement and drama.

As I took a deep breath and sighed, preparing to finally discuss the events of the day with Carl, he glanced at his watch, popped up out of his chair and headed for the door. Before vanishing through the doorway, he turned and cheerfully said, "Same time tomorrow?" As I nodded in acknowledgment, he said, "Just lock up the office when you're finished. See you tomorrow at 8:00."

Again I was caught off guard. Minutes passed before I moved. I was spinning in a surrealistic world, surrounded by the events of the day and by the many toys, objects and artifacts in the office. Following such a draining day, Carl's energy and enthusiasm were unnerving. After all, he was nearing 70. I was not yet 30.

That day convinced me that there was something to be learned from this man. The ensuing years brought continued visits. Each experience was valuable in a different way. When Carl retired from the University of Wisconsin and it was no longer practical to participate in his clinical practice, the notion of passing on some of my learnings came to mind. This book and an accompanying videotape are the results of this idea.

The intent of the book is to present something of clinical importance, not to offer an all-encompassing theory of family therapy. It is my belief that by exploring Carl's work with this one family the core elements of his work will come through. Rather than hurriedly flitting through the museum to be sure you catch a glimpse of each painting, spending time with one masterpiece may offer a deeper understanding and appreciation of the art.

Throughout this text, a dual focus will be emphasized. You will be asked to remain cognizant of the centrality of the person of the therapist, as well as of the evolving process of the therapy. Without this sort of binocular vision, it may be impossible to really integrate the material.

While the transcript material comes directly from Carl's work with the family, the supporting text and theoretical material are shared products. Carl's ideas, as they have impacted me, are expressed through my pen. Those of you who know Carl and his work may feel there are distortions and omissions in the writing. Apologies! I trust you will feel free to further edit this text to make it more useful in your own work. Have fun!

In addition to the efforts of Carl and myself in preparing this book, others made significant contributions. Warmest regards and thanks to Muriel Whitaker for her contributions to numerous discussions related to this project. Deepest appreciation to my wife, Kathy, for her constant encouragement and support, as well as the creative critique that greatly enriched this book.

Thanks are also extended to Steven Tenenbaum for his collaboration in producing the videotape, to Jan Martinson for his professionalism in filming the material, and to my friends at the Family Therapy Institute of Southern California for their support in piloting the tape.

Finally, I would like to express my deepest gratitude to the family. Their selflessness in sharing this part of their lives, so that ours might be enriched, is inspiring. It was a privilege working with them.

W. B.

DANCING WITH THE FAMILY

A
Symbolic-Experiential
Approach

1

Beginning with the Family: Joining, Reframing and Expanding the Symptom

As we settled in for the initial session, there was a sense of tension in the air. John and Marie selected the couch to my right, nervously fidgeting as three of their five adult children found places on the remaining couch. Their two missing offspring would join us for the final day of this three-day experience.

This was obviously a farm family, perhaps similar to the one I grew up in. Dad was decked out in brand new bib overalls, while Mom was neatly but casually attired. Their three daughters, Vanessa aged 30, Doris 27 and Marla 18, were more fashionable and less rural in appearance. As we spent a few minutes engaged in small talk, Vanessa emerged as the family spokesperson.

We briefly reviewed how they had decided to come for these sessions and covered the logistics for our three-day experience. Vanessa had instigated the idea of meeting. She was in the process of studying to become a therapist. Though geographically distant from the rest of the family, she felt tied up by the family struggles and wanted relief. She was also concerned about her 28-year-old sister, Gail. Gail had been hospitalized due to emotional stresses. She had recently entered a halfway house program and was being maintained on medications.

Interestingly, Gail's therapist felt that their current treatment régime was quite successful and opposed her participation in the family sessions, fearing it would jeopardize her progress. Despite the risks, Gail decided to attend the final day, apparently with the blessing of her therapist.

Twenty-three-year-old Mike, the only male among the siblings, was also delayed in arriving. He had work conflicts and was to bring Gail to the sessions. They all lived out of town and had lengthy drives.

5

Beginning

The opening moments of the initial session are often pivotal. The anxiety level far exceeds mere social discomfort. An intense, covert, bilateral sizing-up process instinctively begins. While we frequently mask the undercurrent tensions, they do exist. Questions such as, "What are you really like?" "What are you going to do to me?" and "How far will we be able to go together?" flood into our collective unconscious.

This is a time for establishing some personal connection, not for remaining "professional" and aloof. One of the initial tasks is to let them know something of how I operate and what I expect from them. I need to establish the parameters of my involvement with them and to clarify my conditions for the relationship.

As I take a position, an interactive process is triggered. My action begets their reaction. As they react, I respond to them and an interactive set is under way. Hopefully this dialectic will eventually lead to a higher order synthesis.

Another component in understanding how this works is to consider the very real difference between assertion and aggression. In taking a clear "I" position, I'm not really out to bully them but rather ready to share with them some of my convictions. They, of course, remain free to respond in any fashion they desire. They may balk, rebel, capitulate, or act completely aloof and uninterested. In any event, the process is under way. Rather than the first hour revolving around the revealing pornography of a sterile "assessment interview," we are learning to dance.

In the brief opening segment that follows, notice the political positioning that sets the structure for what is to follow. My intent is to share with them my belief that their willingness to expose their pain is essential to growth in therapy. Additionally, they need to accept the fact that they remain responsible for their own living. Attempting to relinquish control or responsibility to me will do nothing to enhance their living.

Carl: How did you decide to come? What would you like to get out of it? How can I help?

Let me tell you how I deal. I'd like to hear about you to get a sense of the pain you are going through. So I can feel my way into the family. But I need to be clear with you, that I'm sort of a coach on this baseball team, I'm not playing on it. You have to make the final decisions about what you do with your living.

(*pause*)

I should warn you that I get mean.

Being straight with the family about my conditions for working with them is crucial. I want them to understand that while I am willing to work with them, I'm not interested in becoming a real family member.

My responsibility includes being as personally responsive as I can to their pain but does not rest on accepting any responsibility for their real living.

My addendum about being mean is to free them from the cure fantasy they arrived with. I try to contaminate this idea. Merely attending will do them no good. There is hard work ahead. I can't do it for them, or spare them from the struggle.

Dad: We're used to that on the farm.

Carl: You're used to that on the farm? I was born and brought up on a dairy farm. I should have brought my cow! I did a workshop and someone gave me a little toy cow with udders, in case I was feeling lonely and wanted to cuddle up to a cow again.

Dad's reaction to my offer triggered a joining reply on my part. I wanted to let the family know that I too was a farmer. That I might be able to feel for them. That I might be able to relate to them in a personal way regarding their struggles.

This type of joining can be particularly powerful because it's for real. It comes from a common life experience. This is far more personal than the standard professional offer of, "I'd like to help you."

At this point in the interview, Mom seems nervous. She may be concerned that Dad and I will have too much in common. Her automatic reaction is to lodge a slightly disguised complaint against him. If she can discredit him in some way, it may reduce the odds of my being seduced by him. While her concern may have some merit, I was not ready to be drawn into a crossfire at such an early phase.

Mom: He just had to wear his overalls! I said, "Do you think it's OK to wear them to this sort of meeting?"

He had them for six months and wouldn't try them on. Wouldn't even try them on! I was supposed to shorten them. Well, finally I measured them against his old ones and sewed them up last night.

Carl: I've often had the feeling that one of the things I carry over from my childhood is when something would break down, the tractor, the mowing machine or whatever. . . .

Mom: Yes.

Carl: . . . and my dad would come up to the house to get the keys to the car. My mother would say, "Are you going to town? Don't you think you ought to change into a pair of trousers?" and he'd say, "I don't see what's wrong with overalls!" That's about as hot a fight as my parents ever had, as far as I know about.

Mom: Really?

Carl: I have the feeling I'm

still carrying it. That I can
buy a suit and have it looking
like overalls in about three
days.

(*laughter*)

So I'm still fighting with
my mother about wearing
good clothes.

This was an instinctive
reaction to Mom's effort to
seduce me into siding with
her against Dad. She wanted
me to agree with her that Dad
is irresponsible.

Though she was talking
about overalls, the real
implication was clear. This
was a way of defining herself
as not being responsible for
any of their struggles.

We have now completed one cycle of a process that will
repetitively occur throughout the course of therapy. In these
first few moments I have moved to join with them, as well as to
individuate from them. This freedom to move in and move out
is a basic task of the therapy, and of all living. We seek simulta-
neously deeper levels of belonging and individuating.

When we talk about life, we're really talking about relationships. We don't exist in isolation. Emotional living is always
"other" involved.

*   *   *   *   *

Ques: OK Carl, I've got some questions about this segment
right off the bat. What were you trying to accomplish
with this kind of opening? Especially warning them

about your being mean? Is it that you don't care about them or what?

Ans: Of course I don't care about them! I just met them! I hope to come to care about them, because it would be lonesome to sit there and just talk to strangers. But I want them to be clear that I'm not artificially playing host. I'm like any surgeon. I'm interested in getting the pathology resolved, not in preventing the flow of blood. They need to know that it's painful, so they're prepared. Just like a dentist would tell you, "You know this is going to hurt" before he puts the needle in your tooth.

I call this the Battle for Initiative really. It's making them maintain the initiative in their own life. It's making sure that the anxiety they came with stays there. That they don't go anxiety-free and collapse and expect me to handle their world.

Ques: But they're coming to you for some help with their anxiety. That's why they're there! You're saying you're not going to do that?

Ans: That's right! I do not want to relieve their anxiety. I want their anxiety to be the power that makes things move. Then I want to combine with it to make their anxiety more productive.

Ques: Near the end of that segment, you started talking about cows and the farm and that you were from the farm. What was all that about?

Ans: That's a way of what Minuchin calls joining. If you can make common cause. . . .

I think the transference, . . . Freud made a serious mistake, . . . I shouldn't tell him, . . . by assuming the patient's transference is what makes the therapy work. I don't think that's true. I think it's the mother's breastfeeding that makes the child love the mother, not the child's loving the mother that makes the mother have a flow of milk.

I think the therapist needs to internalize the patient's pain so that he identifies with him. So that he gets an empathetic response in himself. Then he has to be very careful that he's not sucked into taking over.

*   *   *   *   *

Searching for Father

Early in the initial session I typically engage the family in a history-taking process. This is not just a history that surrounds the presenting problem. Quite the opposite is true. I'm out to learn more about the family as a whole. By pushing for an overall picture of the family, I'm letting them know that I view them through a different lens. I'm telling them that I'm interested in all of them. That I really don't accept their sacrificial victim as the star.

This sort of family history paints a richer context from which to operate. Some of the core sources of the family pain and struggles are revealed. Three-generational patterning begins to come into focus. Their mythology regarding issues such as death, illness, rage and divorce comes to light. This broadens the family frame. It also provides the opportunity to address some affectively loaded areas in a nonthreatening way. The family is asked to be personal right off the bat. Since this is our initial meeting, they don't develop the undercurrent sense of paranoia that emerges out of a sense of having been figured out or discovered beforehand.

My standard starting point is to begin with Dad. In our culture, the father is typically the more peripheral parent. It's my intention to engage him immediately.

Rather than it being an act of deference to the man as the head of the household, I'm challenging his position of being a nonperson, a nonmember of the family. I've often had the experience of seeing the father not so much as a family member but as the man who lives next door. He's like a person coming home for food or sex, but not to be included as an intimate. Challenging this pseudoposition is central to creating a sense of the family unit. It's difficult to arrive at a sense of family nationalism when Dad is physically present but emotionally absent. By bringing him into the discussion, I'm offering the family a sense of hope that life can really change.

Carl: Dad, can you tell me about the family? Not the people in it, but how it operates.

Dad: Well, nowadays it's difficult on the farm. There's a lot of outside interference and . . . oh, I might say competition.

Then, of course, whoever is stuck on the farm or has to operate it . . . well, you just don't like that. You resent it. You try to keep the place going. One thing leads to another and they leave, sometimes not in the best humor. The only time they come back is for a visit.

Fathers typically have a very difficult time responding to this sort of question. While Dad's response was somewhat vague, it didn't seem to be evasive. He identified areas of tension and revealed an awareness of dissatisfaction.

As Dad's description of the family continued, he also listed the ages of all the children. In discussing Marla, the youngest of the children, he began with, "Here's the baby." Perhaps it was the fact that this introduction seemed more personal that led me to comment on it.

Carl: You don't look very babyish from here. Change the word to babe nowadays I suppose.

Dad: Yes. She's quite a babe too, if you want to put it that way.

Carl: Well, I wasn't wanting to put it that way since you were here. You know. You have to be careful when the old man is around.

Dad: Yes.

(*laughter*)

This was a rather covert way of probing about an undercurrent of sexuality that I sensed but couldn't identify.

A few minutes later Dad's description of the family resumed. Of note here was the need to address Mom directly. She was becoming uncomfortable with so much focus on Dad. Given her status as the emotional hub of the family, it's difficult for her to tolerate too much of his input.

Carl: Tell me about how the family was in the old days, Dad.
     Mom, can you let me talk

to Dad first so I can get some
sense of how he thinks of it?

Mom: OK.

> While this appears to be an almost incidental sort of comment, it has a clear purpose. I'm letting Mom know that I haven't forgotten about her, as well as telling her not to interfere in my discussion with her husband.

Dad continued on, speaking of the interpersonal dynamics among the five children, as well as underscoring a clear division of labor model regarding the marriage. A lack of real unity between the parents concerning child rearing practices was clear. He noted that often their lack of consistency left the children confused.

Shifting Perspectives: Creating an Interactive Set

As the interview process turned to address family-of-origin type issues, the tension was more pronounced. In this vignette, historical information will be brought to bear on the present. It will candidly reveal much about the current state of the spousal relationship. As we join the vignette, I am questioning Dad about his parents.

Carl: Is he dead, too?

Dad: Yes.

Carl: When did he die?

Dad: In 1972.

Carl: What was wrong?

Dad: He was 89 years old.

Infirmity and old age. He
lived a pretty good life.

Carl: And Mom? . . . Was
Dad a farmer, too?

Dad: Yes.

Carl: What did Mother die
of?

Dad: She died at 62 of pneu-
monia. We could have avoided
it if we had realized it.

Carl: And what about Dad?
Did he remarry?

Dad: No.

Carl: How many brothers and
sisters?

Dad: None.

Carl: You're the only child?
No wonder you're spoiled,
huh?

Mom: That's it!

Carl: That's the real problem,
huh?

As the history unfolded, I was
suddenly taken by this bit of
data. Perhaps it seemed
unusual in a farm family. My
response was mindless, in the
sense of having no clear
purpose, but it was highly
relevant in terms of representing my internal association to
the data as it emerged.

The capacity to sense and

utilize these associations is central to my work. Moving from the data that Dad was an only child to calling him spoiled was an automatic reaction, not a planned intervention.

The sharing of my association was also significant in the reply it elicited from Mom. The inference was that she sees herself as an innocent victim of his insensitivity.

Mom: Yes. If he had been brought up . . . he would have had a sister. Really! A sister that wouldn't have been that different in age. Molly was walking in the milkhouse one day and slipped. She lost the baby at 8 months.

Dor: Older or younger?

Mom: She would have been younger. It would have been good because she would have told him, "Get out of here! Don't do that!" Brothers and sisters will tell each other. Friends are afraid.

Carl: Is that true of wives, too, or are you being a good sister to him?

Mom: Maybe I am. Maybe I'm too good to him.

Carl: Why don't you get over that?

In an effort to mobilize Mom to be more direct, I've personalized this issue to clearly reflect on her.

Mom: I don't know! It's hard for me.

Carl: Just a sucker are you? . . . Just naturally?

Mom: What? What did you say?

Carl: Are you just a natural-born sucker?

In order to free Mom from her self-defined role as victim to her husband's lack of attention, I've labeled her as a sucker. I'm suggesting that there is something stupid about taking it.

Now the picture can be more complex than a mere inept husband. Now she too fits into the puzzle, forming a complete gestalt of marital mutuality.

Mom: Maybe I am! Oh, I get mad at him a lot of times, but he just walks away. He won't fight! He walks to the back 40 (acres) and I can't find him. I get mad because he won't fight it out. He just walks away!

Here Mom reveals that she realizes that her approach isn't working. She persists with ineffective responses. She claims to want change but feels helpless because her husband won't cooperate. She lives with an external locus of control.

Carl: Why don't you get a bow
and arrow or something?

Dor: Take the tractor.

Carl: Or a shotgun full of rock
salt? They used to talk about
that when I was a kid.

In order to counter her
continued helplessness, I've
decided to amplify the situation. I'm trying to call her to
action with more intensity by
suggesting the use of a bow
and arrow. It's my hope that
this will help her realize there
are more ways to try. I want
to empower her! I'm also
saying that I won't collude
with her self-victimization. In
a funny way, I'm offering
hope.

*   *   *   *   *

Ques: Carl, what are you trying to accomplish here? Why did
you so quickly label Dad as spoiled and Mom as a sucker? What are you really up to?

Ans: It wasn't so quickly. I set up Father in his lifestyle by
finding out about his father and mother and miscarried
sister. I found that he was an only child and said what I
believe about only children, that they marry someone
who's going to keep them spoiled. Then I accused Mother of being a sucker.

In doing it in this kind of meta way, I set it up for them
to each be victim to the other and to each be dominant on
the other. So that I have an interactional system. I'm
already talking about systems, rather than individuals.

Ques: But the way you did that then. . . . It's like you took an
idea from your own head, from your own thinking, and

you imposed it on them. Isn't that dangerous? I mean, you weren't using information from the interview!

Ans: No. I think it's the other way around! If you take it from them, then it's dangerous because then they have to fight you. If you produce your own ideas, then they can dump it, or keep it, or adopt it later. It's not their responsibility, it's yours!

Ques: But isn't it a risky thing to do professionally? To bring yourself front and center into the room like that? Aren't you supposed to do an assessment first?

Ans: I don't believe that! I think doing an assessment is apt to be pornographic. It comes about out of our own patholo-gy and our own curiosity. I think the best way to do it is to make a judgment and let them decide whether your judg-ment is right or wrong. That keeps them in a respected position, rather than degraded by your being a detective and a peeping Tom and they're supposed to be exhibi-tionistic.

*   *   *   *   *

This segment points to another crucial aspect of working with families. When I meet with a family, I am absolutely certain they have within themselves the capacity to struggle and grow. There is no need to assess or evaluate this. I know it is possible. The real question becomes one of courage, both theirs and mine. Are we willing to take the risk of sailing into un-charted waters?

This family entered with the unspoken assumption that Dad is the real problem. That his inability to talk and be supportive is the key. It is perceived as his unwillingness to get involved, rather than as a broader family problem with involvement and intimacy. I want to free them from this narrow logic and create hope by developing alternative perspectives. In this particular example, the mother is the other side of the coin. Her power must be activated for real change to begin. By framing together the concepts of a "spoiled" child and a "sucker," it is possible to look at their relationship as a skillfully choreographed dance. One in which they move in perfect synchrony. By defining the power as mutually owned and shared, both are free to initiate the process of transformation.

But it takes more! Not only must the old model be destroyed and their mutuality highlighted but it must be done in a way that is not easily repudiated. Offering Mother the fantasy image of hunting Dad down with a bow and arrow may serve to empower her. It leaves her with the message that there are things she could try. At the same time, of course, Dad is being warned to be a bit more wary. If Mother actually begins to take herself and her needs more seriously, her husband may be forced to follow suit. The bow and arrow metaphor is a wonderful way of encouraging her to take herself more seriously without running the risk of my taking her more seriously than she does.

As the session continued, the theme of emotional distance between Mom and Dad persisted. While Mom complained, she seemed resigned to it. She continued to view it as his decision and to feel victimized by his indifference.

As in the previous segment, my efforts are to help her shed the skin of linear logic. I want to thrust her into a world of mutuality and bilateral determination. This theme will repetitively surface, as it has served as a real pillar in their homeostatic balance. Much like the dilemma of Chinese handcuffs, in order to break the impasse she must be willing to abandon a position she tenaciously holds. She must face the fact of her full partnership in the struggle.

As in the previous vignette, note the effort to frame their dance as one requiring mutual cooperation. It's not one *or* the other, it's one *and* the other. They have mutually created a lifestyle that precludes marital intimacy.

Carl: How long after you were married before you decided

With this comment, I'm attempting to provide an

he loved the cows more than he did you?

absurd metaphor that will stay with them. I'm offering a new way of looking at the facts of their living. The image of Dad embracing the cows will remain with them long after our sessions have ended.

Mom: Well . . . I don't know. I can't remember. I had one kid after the other. It's hard. I don't know.

Carl: What did he substitute when you started loving the kids instead of him? Loving money or just the cows?

By identifying a parallel process of her infidelity, a more complete gestalt is formed. I want them to clearly see the course their marriage has taken.

Mom: Loving work probably.

Carl: Just work, huh?

*   *   *   *   *

Ques: Well, I can see the mutuality here, Carl. I can see that they are together, that they're both part of this whole thing. But you know, the image of Dad caressing the cows and Mom the kids. . . . What a crazy image that is!

Ans: That's a very critical business! If you talk about something that's so crazy that they can't fit it into their programmed thinking process, then you leave them with a picture that's yours, not theirs, and they can begin to attach symbolism to it. They can begin to attach power to it, until it becomes a very loaded part of their life.

Ques: Do farmers really fall in love with their cows rather than with their wives?

Ans: Of course! They have 60 cows and they can name every one of them.

*   *   *   *   *

This segment exposes a pervasive, culturally sanctioned variety of marital infidelity. The bilateral infidelity of Dad falling in love with his work and Mom with the kids is rampant.

In uncovering this sort of dynamic, I often make a point of labeling emotional betrayals of the marriage as affairs. While this word typically is associated with a sexual connotation, I endeavor to broaden the definition. I want to establish it as an emotional giving of your heart to someone or something other than your spouse. It's important to help marital partners realize that there are many ways to fall away from each other. I want them to appreciate the notion that significant investment elsewhere can drain the vitality from the marriage.

While the sexual variety of infidelity often carries with it a special sense of resentment and bitterness, nonsexual affairs are also powerful. By desexualizing the word "affair," I hope to transform it into a description that becomes part of the couple's thinking in day-to-day life. When successful, it seems to have the effect of raising their level of consciousness concerning how they treat each other.

The usual developmental scenario for this bilateral infidelity goes as follows. As mother's pregnancy with the firstborn progresses, she becomes more and more involved with her child. She and the child become one, while the father, no matter how involved, is somewhat more distant. After birth, the mother/child affair continues, with Dad still on the outside. Feeling rejected and abandoned, he may turn elsewhere for love. He is "at risk" for overinvesting in his work, his golf game, or the secretary. The maturity to remain focused on the family seems lacking. Few men have the capacity to hold their breath and wait for the mother/infant symbiosis to loosen so they can more fully enter.

During this transitional period of changing from a couple to a family, the massive developmental tasks at hand often overwhelm the couple. Unless they successfully find their way back to each other, while also incorporating the baby, the marriage is in jeopardy. They either grow together or grow apart; there is no neutral course.

Continuing on with the previous segment, an interesting dichotomy arises. The complexities of being a mother to a husband are exposed.

Carl: Is he a real workaholic?
Just loves work and nothing
else?

Mom: Yes.

Carl: He can't enjoy play?

Mom: Oh, he can! He can
dance real good.

Carl: Really?

Mom: Yes. He's an excellent
dancer. He can roller-skate
too. He's handy. Women love
him. All women love him!

Carl: Except the ones that are
married to him.

Mom: Yes. That's right.

(*laughter*)

Carl: You might have to
change places with some of
them. Then you could love

him and they could take care
of him.

Mom: Yes. That's it! They
don't realize what it is to live
with him. I tell him, "Oh,
you're hard to live with, Dad.
You're so demanding."

Carl: You call him Dad. I
thought he'd call you Mom.

Mom: He doesn't.

Carl: He doesn't call you
Mom? He just expects you to
keep on being his mother,
huh?

Here we're directly discussing
the fact that relationships can
be viewed from a variety of
angles. We're talking about
the difference of being a wife
to a husband or a mother to a
little boy. While both roles
may be part of real relationships, one must take dominance.

The discussion shifted to the family's decision to not ask the
maternal grandmother to attend the sessions. Dad was the
family member most in favor of inviting her, while Mom was
the most clearly opposed.

The following segment reveals some of the complicated dynamics that permeate the family.

Carl: I just had a crazy idea.
Do you ever have crazy ideas?
I have this theory, I have
theories coming out of my
ears. One of them is that you
fall in love with the mother
and then marry the daughter.

Did you ever think of that?
That he fell in love with your
mother and then married
you?

Mom: Yes, because they get
along just perfect.

(*laughter*)

We come into the house
and she runs up and goes,
"Oh, John!" She grabs him!

Carl: Does he take her to
dances?

Mom: No.

Carl: Do you dance, too?

Mom: Yes, but not as good
as . . .

Carl: Not as good as your
mother, huh?

Mom: Well, she's pretty good
on her feet. She's a lot more
limber than I am.

Carl: Maybe that's why you
haven't run away from the
marriage in all these years.
You can't take on your
mother.

Mom: We're so close knit, you
can't.

Carl: You mean it's a kind of bigamy? Is he married to both of you?

Mom: Yes. He probably is.

This is important. It's now clear that Dad can be close with people. It's just that he and his wife are distant.

Later in the session, the focus shifted to the topic of Dad's old girlfriends. This led to another opportunity to assault Mom's tendency to not take herself more seriously. By challenging this, I try to help her become more of a person. This would provide impetus for the full family to take the risk to grow.

Mom: Dad still talks about his old girlfriends.

Carl: Do they ever come back to compete with you?

Mom: Yes. He throws them back at me all the time.

Carl: Do you ever worry about where he goes when he goes to town?

Mom: No.

Carl: You think he's too old, huh?

Mom: No. I just think he's . . . I trust him.

Carl: You trust him? Well, good lord! That's crazy! Can you imagine that? A woman trusting a man.

Mom: Well, I trust him because I don't do anything that I shouldn't.

Carl: She's still a sucker.

Dor: Yes.

Mom: Maybe I am a sucker.

Carl: Yes. Trusting a man! Anybody who trusts a man is a sucker!

Here I'm trying to contaminate Mom's comfort with her deadened view of her marriage. What she is calling trust may, of course, really be a lack of interest.

This was fun! It was an opportunity to speak tongue-in-cheek, and yet to be straight at the same time. By teasing Mom about trusting Dad, I'm also challenging the full family to reevaluate the idea of trust.

Father Begins to Emerge

As the initial session began to wind down, the focus again turned to Dad. This time the discussion centered on the issue of his unhappiness. He was described as being burnt out on farm work and the heavy toll it demanded.

Carl: How about that, Mom? Do you think Dad burned out 10 years ago?

Mom: Well, I don't know what you mean by burned out.

Carl: Fed up! Has had it with that job. Ready for a change. I guess if I were to say it openly, feeling suicidal. You know. Over the top of the hill and waiting for death to catch up with you.

Mom: I don't know. He always sort of talked of stuff like that. He was morbid. He liked funerals. Now he doesn't like to go anymore.

Carl: He doesn't like funerals anymore?

Mom: No. He doesn't like to go. He wants to move so he doesn't have to go to his friends' funerals.

Carl: When did he change?

Mom: A year ago. He said, "Let's go to California. Then we wouldn't have to go to all of their funerals."

Carl: Do you feel lonesome, Dad?

Dad: Yes.

The progression from feeling burned out to talking of his loneliness is encouraging. It suggests that he may be able to face his need for others.

Carl: How much longer do you think you're going to live?

Dad: Well, that's a good question. As far as I'm concerned, I'm ready any day.

Carl: Oh really?

Dad: Sure.

Carl: Why?

Dad: I lived a good life. I did everything I ever wanted to

do. If I lived it again, I'd do it
the same.

Carl: You wouldn't do it 10
more times?

Dad: Well, . . . how could
you?

Carl: Well, I wasn't going to
talk about me. Just about
you.

Dad: Well, if I lived it over, I'd
go the same way. I have no
regrets. It was hard work, but
one thing with it, you always
had the satisfaction of seeing
your accomplishments. While
with a lot of things, a good
factory job for instance, you
get good money but you have
nothing to show for it. But on
the farm, if you're lucky and
have a good crop, you can
take care of your food and
clothes. You have no debt and
no credit.

Carl: I just had a funny
feeling. Is he a softy? I
thought he was going to cry.

Mom: He never cries at
funerals, or anything. Even at
his Dad's funeral. I was
sobbing away.

Dor: He did at the end.

Mom: Yes, I saw him at the end. A teeny bit.

Dor: Well, we all have our levels.

Carl: I thought he was going to cry just now. Did you feel like crying a minute ago?

Dad: Well, I feel . . . sometimes I get that way. You know, but . . . Well, like with my Dad. If you had seen what he went through. I was glad he could go.

Again, being able to label Dad as a human being rather than a machine is crucial. Establishing the fact that he, too, has feelings is vital.

As the opening session ends, Dad has begun to show signs of humanness and the marital relationship has been redefined as a joint partnership. The undercurrent sense of a protagonist and antagonist has been replaced by a more fluid model. Their interactive nature is now highlighted.

2

Person of the Therapist: Personal Integrity and Professional Role Structure

The process of family therapy revolves around people and relationships, not intervention techniques or theoretical abstractions. The therapist, as a human being, is pivotal. As Betz and Whitehorn (1975) so nicely put it, "The dynamics of psychotherapy lies in the person of the therapist." Theory and technique come alive and take form only when filtered through the personhood of a therapist.

As people who also happen to be therapists, we would be foolish not to take seriously the centrality of our personhood, philosophical assumptions, and personal biases to the process of therapy. Our beliefs about the nature of human beings, the power of relationships, and the essence of the therapist's role are guides that direct our actions, often without conscious consent.

If psychotherapy is really to be a human encounter, it requires a therapist who has retained the capacity to be a person. As a professional therapist you must care enough to get in and get involved, while retaining enough love of self to withstand the cultural mandate of sacrificing yourself to save the family. The societal assumption that you should be able to save every family that stumbles into your office is deadly. To be a savior, you must also request a crown of thorns. While compassion is essential, the professional therapist cannot hope to be helpful, let alone to survive, if too swayed by altruism. In this sense, becoming a missionary serves well only the cannibals . . . at least for that one glorious meal.

To be useful to a family in distress, a therapist must be clear concerning the professional role structure he will embrace. The role we settle on speaks eloquently of our own personhood, as well as of our views of others. I consider a basic guide to my professional role to be that of maximizing the growth of all involved in the therapeutic process, including my own. Perhaps most importantly my own. Only by remaining cognizant of my own need to grow and desire to avoid burnout is my capacity to be useful to others preserved. But it's more than a preventative function. My capacity to be real, to be alive during the session, to respond in a personal fashion is the essence of what I have to offer. This requires that I get something out of it too. There's really no such thing as pure altruism.

Personal Integrity

It seems too crazy, even for me, to try to say something to you about your personhood. So let me say something about my "belief system." Let me share with you some of my assumptions and biases as a way of conveying something personal about my work with families. This "belief system," as I've come to call it, lies at the core of any therapist's work.

The first assumption to grapple with is your basic view of people. How do you see them? What prompts them to act as they do? Why do they treat each other as they do? After more than 40 years in this crazy business, I've finally come to realize that I don't believe in people. There's really no such thing as an individual. We're all just fragments of families floating around, trying to live life. All of life and all of pathology is interpersonal. Focusing on intrapsychic processes within a particular person is merely a way of simplifying life beyond reality. Given this perspective, I naturally choose to work with families. That's where the real power and energy of life are found.

Families are not fragile. They are robust and resilient. We should probably be less worried about being too influential with them. Perhaps a more justifiable concern centers on our inability to reach them in any significant way. When a family enters a therapist's office, they have already decided what the problems are, who is at fault, and what needs to be done to correct them. As Mark Twain is reputed to have said, "Even the town drunk is an elected office." In the drama of life, families create the roles, assign the parts, and direct the action. In one sense, we're much like the first-year film student who recommends sweeping changes in the favorite script of an Oscar-winning director. Who listens?

When a family approaches a therapist, all members want their personal views validated. While this is their desire, it is not what they need. What is needed is an experience that will free them from the blocked perspectives they have developed. They need the opportunity to see their family in a more complicated light. To shed the distorting good-vs.-bad dichotomies they have regressed to. In effect, they need to have their comfort disrupted. They need to be freed to develop the kind of anxiety required to fuel them in a massive growth effort. I've come to think of this as a high-grade sort of fertilizer. While it may not smell good, it's needed for optimal growth. Ask any farmer.

I'm comfortable pushing the family because of my belief that they have unlimited potential. They have the capacity to expand and progress, if only they have the courage to try. My job is to struggle to mobilize that courage. To let them see that conflicts and differences of opinion need not be disastrous. That the only way out of the proverbial wet paper bag is to start swinging. But it's more than a naive "nothing ventured, nothing gained" viewpoint. Families do care about each other! They do have deep emotional investments! They do need each other!

Not to push, under the assumption that it might make things worse, is to decide for the family that they're too sick to care and too inept to grow. These are dangerous assumptions. They reflect a dehumanizing position. To my way of thinking, they're just not true.

It's a tricky business, though. While it's my job to push, it's not my job or my right to tell them how to grow. Trying to sell them my model for living would merely undermine their resources, their capacities. They need to discover their own formula, not try to imitate mine. This whole business of "helping" them is really quite terrifying. It's demeaning to try to "help" them because it suggests that your way of living is superior to theirs. Given the many therapists I've known, myself included, I see no evidence for this assumption. To put it succinctly, "helping doesn't help."

Therapists really don't have the power to inflict growth on a family. You can't tell them how to be more real. Your impact can really only come from the personal process you participate in with them. If you can learn to get in and get out when working with a family, they'll come away with something of value. They'll learn something about the process of individuating and belonging. If you lose yourself and fail to be both caring and tough, no one will stand to gain.

Another way to put it is to say that families don't grow because of something the therapist does to them. Real growth is something the therapist and the family do with each other. It's not the family *or* the therapist, but the family *and* the therapist that make up the vehicle to growth.

What makes this such a foreign notion is that it implies that "we" are no different from "them." That we are more similar to than different from the families we treat. If this is true, then what is it that we have to offer? How do we operate when stripped of the guru's robe or the savior's garment? The role of the expert or guru has a certain appeal because it deceives us into feeling that we're special. That we have the wisdom or intelligence to let "them" know something more about living life. It's seductive, but deadly. After all, the odds are that you'll die too. I'm even coming around to the notion that I'll not survive forever.

The really treacherous part of this is that even if we've been able to catch a glimpse of our own frailty and humanness, the families we see may be determined to see us as all-knowing. It then becomes our responsibility to puncture this delusion. We must let them know that we can't really show them the way. That in order to get anywhere they'll need to get their hands dirty. My favorite way of doing this is to reveal slivers of my own humanness. To encourage them to recognize some of my limitations. A standard retort to a request to tell them what to do with their life is, "I wouldn't begin to know what to tell you to do about your situation. I've got enough problems keeping up with my own life. But I'd be happy to try to be of some utility as you wrestle with your living."

Once you get through all the business of your own grandiosity and the flip side of being a nobody by offering yourself to everybody, you're ready to consider what caring really involves. To be a truly caring therapist, or person for that matter, you need to be able to walk a tightrope. While the capacity to be nurturing is central, the capacity to be tough is equally essential. Being good at either one just doesn't cut it. Excessive nurturing typically falls into the trap of "helping," while exaggerated toughness often is sadistic. Both components of the nurture-toughness duality must exist in some balance. You can really only confront to the extent that you can nurture.

It's much like the dilemma faced by all parents. You must be able to encourage and support, as well as discipline, your children. Finding a good balance is difficult; remaining at that level is impossible. It has been said that it's not really a question of succeeding or failing in raising your children. That's not the choice. The real choice you have is how you are going to fail. Will you be too strict or too soft? Too controlling or too flexible? No matter how you slice it, failing is part of the job. Yet the task of finding a workable balance persists.

Your willingness to bring more and more of yourself to the sessions is the catalytic ingredient that can trigger the family's growth experience. It's a wonderful learning when a family can finally accept that your caring can be tough as well as gentle. And it is even more profound when they realize that despite your caring for them, you care about yourself even more. While it may come as a shock to any vestiges of the guru delusion, it's also a relief. It relieves them from needing to be concerned about taking care of you. Once released from this underreported burden, the family is free to focus on their own needs.

Finally, we should understand that by virtue of the intensity and depth the family brings we are likely to have an intense countertransference reaction. This far surpasses what is typical in individual therapy. Actually, I've now come to think of it as co-transference, meaning it's more of a real transference than merely a reactive countertransference. Conversely, the family members, by virtue of their physical presence as a unit, typically react more profoundly to each other than to the therapist.

These assumptions, or biases if you will, really come out of my beliefs about people. They have very little to do with any sort of theoretical constructs. In fact, I really don't believe that theories we read about have much to do with our assumptive base. I think it works the opposite way — that we find theories that fit in with our biases. When we stumble onto an idea we like, we automatically run it through our computer. If it fits with our programming, we claim it. If not, we reject it as being wrong, or at least not useful.

Use of Self

Prior to fortifying ourselves with the armor of theories and techniques that offer protection when our courage fails, it's vital to peek into our world of values and biases. This is especially so if the primary tool of any therapist is himself.

In a way, this suggests that we all must reinvent the wheel in order to be therapists. We must grapple with life and with ourselves until we can see beneath the surface. We must have some connection with and access to our own impulses, intuitions and associations. Only when you've struggled with yourself are you free to bring your person, not just your therapist's uniform, into the therapy room.

One of the real dangers in our field is to look too intensely for external facts that will enable you to be a therapist. It's important to realize that we filter and organize these "facts" through our own internal mechanisms. This allows them to fit into our personalized bias system. Remember, I can see you only through the me I know. I can understand *your* family only through the filter of *my* family. My self search, then, is central to my use of self.

One of the early cues as to how well I'll be able to work with a particular family is the extent to which I can see myself in them. This has some prognostic value concerning how fully I'll be able to really "get in," or empathize with them. If I can really see myself in their struggles, we've got a chance. If, however, they seem too different, too alien, we've got a problem. If our worlds are too different, adding a cotherapist who more intimately knows their world can be invaluable. Severe cultural dissonance need not preclude therapy, but you need to take it seriously.

In a similar vein, if I notice that I'm having a hard time caring about a particular family, it's a good idea to let them know about it. Responding with, "You know, I'm having a hard time in hearing anything personal from you. I'm not getting any sense of your pain. If you could get more personal, maybe I could feel more involved," can bring a session to life.

Any therapy that is useful involves a certain amount of agony and struggle. As the family strives to reach new territories, the terrain becomes treacherous. In order for them to really risk the journey, they must come to accept the idea that pain is not the enemy. It's more of a companion. It's really my capacity to care about them, to invest in them, that helps make it tolerable. If they sense my caring, they'll consider the journey. Otherwise, they're wise to pull out.

Personal confrontation, of course, is the other side of personal caring. You're only able to love to the extent that you're free to hate. As Winnicott (1949) once said, "If you haven't been hated by your therapist, you've been cheated." Personal confrontation is a valuable experience. It's an event that enlivens all of us. I want "them" to have to face "me." It gets the blood flowing. It's the experience that's important, not the outcome.

Just as it is in marriage, a relationship that has an understructure of caring can be enriched and enhanced by confrontation. One lacking this foundation will crumble. Perhaps it's even easier in the therapeutic than in the marital arena. As a therapist, my investment is in being involved in a real experience with the family, not in trying to change them. The confrontation is more of a sharing of perspective, not a manipulation. My effort is to be honest with them, leaving them free to decide what to do with it. Let me give you an example of this kind of sharing.

Halfway through the initial interview with a family, the session had gone flat. Since they had stopped, I found myself thinking about a problem I was having with my sailboat. The following exchange occurred.

Dad: Well, what should we talk about? You're the expert here.

Ther: It's funny that you ask. I was just sitting here thinking about what to do about a problem I'm having with my sailboat. The shackle is broken and I haven't been able to fix it.
(*pause*)

Mom: You're bored, too, huh? For the last 10 minutes I've been bored to death and wondering what we're hiding from.

The crazy thing about this was that I didn't even realize I was bored. When Mom labeled it, I realized she was right. My automatic honesty in this situation led the family back to the issue of their taking responsibility. It moved them away from their fantasy dependency on me to teach them.

Another of my beliefs is that when meeting with a family, any ideas, thoughts, or associations that break into my consciousness belong to them as much as to me. It's the combined therapist-family supraset that arouses these notions or images. As such, it seems only appropriate to consider sharing them with the family. Of course, my awareness of these associations is tied to how well I know myself. To how free I am to tune in to my own internal processes.

Here are a few examples.

"You know, that little smile that snuck across your face when you said you never thought of cheating on your wife? Well, I had a crazy association to it. It reminded me of the little boy who got caught with his hand in the cookie jar. I wonder why those cookies always taste better?"

"The way you two so carefully stay away from each other would sure scare me. I'd expect you to be tempted to try to find an affair. At least you could delude yourself for a while with pseudo-intimacy."

"You know, the way your little boy fights so intensely against Daddy reminded me of a biblical story. I had the strange association that you had raised little David to slay Goliath."

Responsibility of the Therapist

One of the most troublesome areas for therapists is that of sorting out what their responsibility is to the family they're working with. This is a tricky area because of the implicit, unspoken assumptions that underscore the positions adopted. The more a therapist feels the need to take responsibility for a client, the less he believes in the client's capacity to be a competent person. We should avoid convincing people that they're inept. For example, I've long balked at the idea of calling a child's teacher to discuss his behavior problem. The basic reason is that I don't want to reinforce the idea that the parents are stupid. They're the ones who need to talk with the teacher, not me. They know their child better than I ever will. They love their child more than I ever could.

It's my posture to strive to be responsive *to* the family without being responsible *for* them. I deal with them at an "as if" or symbolic level, never taking a real life role. My goal is to be as personally responsive as I can. I want to have a human interchange occur. But I am careful to avoid any covert effort on their part to abdicate responsibility for their living. It's their game, not mine. In effect, it's my responsibility to push them to accept full responsibility for their living.

The other area of my responsibility lies in a more technical or theoretical area. Given my particular biases and beliefs about people and what growth entails, I must make some professional decisions. At this point in my career I'm more focused on optimal, rather than marginal growth. I therefore take it as my responsibility to stack the deck in favor of change. I want to create the conditions that will enhance the possibility of real growth. Temporary relief or minor changes that will be of no real impact are of little interest.

This stacking of the deck requires that the full family attend the session. I see the family organism as the real source of power and influence. To not take this seriously is to create a situation where any growth may really be pseudo-growth. The broader family network can easily undo it and return to their homeostatic balance. In this area, I need to be the one who takes responsibility. It's much like the surgeon who needs certain instruments before beginning a serious operation. I would be foolish to start without the possibility of a successful venture. The presence of the full family is the only way I know to generate sufficient anxiety and motivation for change.

While each family situation may merit an individual evaluation of what your "minimum conditions" are before beginning, be wary of accepting too little. It is better to fail to start than to start and fail. I endeavor to get them to take their own emotional life seriously. But it's imperative that I not take them more seriously than they're willing to take themselves.

The bottom line is that I must accept full responsibility for the decisions I make and the actions I take.

Professional Role Structure

In addition to the myriad of personal factors that influence the way we are therapeutically, a more formalized professional model also comes into play. The professional training we receive and the ideas and values we encounter via books, courses and supervisors all contribute to this evolving model. While it may be difficult to define this model in the abstract, it becomes abundantly clear when we look at our day-to-day clinical functioning.

One of the initial issues to address is that of defining what a therapist is. How do you define your professional role and function? What are you willing to do? How will you choose to respond in various clinical situations? There is really no prepackaged clinical model you can adopt. Your idiographic interpretation of the ideas of others creates your unique brand. Let's examine this issue.

I've come to think of the therapist's role as being a sort of parenting position. Perhaps more of a pseudo-parenting function, because I'm never quite so invested that I'm there in a real-world sense. I'm not really willing to take the family home with me when they need a place to stay. I've been in on the raising of my own children and am not in the market for more. My involvement is more in the realm of a symbolic parent.

Perhaps the idea of a foster parent describes it best. A therapist certainly lacks the primitive identification bond of a biological parent. While he can care about them, it's generally clear that he's not really part of them. Aside from this biologic component, even the role of an adoptive parent is too great. My investment has more limitations than that role invokes. But the foster parent image fits. The limits are clear and agreed upon up front. I'm offering to get involved, but I retain the option of deciding I want out. It's not a lifetime commitment. Lastly, there's an exchange of money. This makes it clear that our arrangement is not one of unrestrained altruism.

From this basic model, it's easier to avoid the temptation of being coopted into a spouse, lover or sibling role. It needs to be clear that I belong to a different generation. That I'm operating at a meta-level to their living. When I feel a pull to fill a different role, I quickly move to expose and contaminate it. During a recent session with an impassed couple, such an issue surfaced.

Wife: Well, Dr., what do you think? You've heard all about our problems and see how unhappy I am. You must have worked with other couples in similar situations. Do you think it would be wise to divorce him?

Ther: Well, I wouldn't know about that. I'm not really available though. I've been married 47 years and am not ready to leave my wife for you. I don't believe in polygamy either.

My reply is intended to both expose the manipulative undercurrent and underscore the absurdity of asking someone else to run your life.

The basic idea of joining also merits a closer look in working with families. While it's a relatively straightforward issue to be able to empathize and offer support to an individual in distress, it's much more complicated with a family. Any comment you make is heard and filtered through a number of ears. A move to be empathic with a wife is heard by the husband as you being duped into believing her side of the story. Letting a parent know that raising children is tough tells the children you're on the enemy's side. The examples of this sort of selective misunderstanding are pervasive.

The solution is to let them know that you've taken the family unit as your focal point. That you have no interest in being aligned with or against any individual member or subgroup. That you are pushing the entire family to grow.

One of the basic things we're hired for as therapists is to be honest. No one really needs phony support. Being a psychological prostitute may offer some level of tainted comfort, but it's not the real thing. Part of the role, then, is to establish a set where you develop the freedom to be straight with them, without being judgmental. When you confront the family, you do it out of a sense of your own honesty, not with the intent of getting them to acquiesce to it. My saying, "I don't think you're being honest," is quite different from saying, "You're a liar." I'm not accusing or trying to sell a point, only sharing my impression.

Dad: I resent that! We came to you because we're worried that Johnny will make another attempt at taking his life. Now you're trying to convince us that he's doing these crazy things to keep me from killing his mother? That's ridiculous!

Ther: Well, I'm just trying to be honest with you. I take it that you don't get that very often.

To my way of thinking the family is playing with fire. They all seem to live in fear of your explosiveness. Especially your wife. Johnny has found a way to get you to look at the possible consequences should it get out of hand.

Dad: That's absurd!

Ther: Sorry about that. But I take it as my job to be straight with you. I'm not interested in joining the list of those who fear you and therefore lie to you.

The issue of confidentiality is another component of this role structure. My belief is that there can be no confidentiality among family members. My role is to facilitate their struggle to grow. Being a repository for secrets and being seduced into covert alliances do not fit with this role. There is a cost, though, to taking such a position. You have to be able to tolerate the idea that family members may decide to withhold "crucial" information from you. They may prefer to be deceptive rather than have it public knowledge in the family. Meeting only with the family can, of course, minimize the opportunities for such maneuvering. But the issue frequently surfaces in different ways. Telephone calls, letters, or unscheduled drop-ins are familiar to all therapists.

The bottom line goes something like this. There are no data so valuable as to convince me to enter into a collusive arrangement with one member of the family versus another. Being available to such political maneuvering may effectively invalidate you as a potentially helpful person. For example, if you agree to speak with a husband in confidence and he tells you he's involved in an affair, what do you do when you meet with the couple? If you tell his wife, you betray his confidence. If you stick with the confidentiality agreement with the husband, you're covertly colluding with him against her. When she then says that she feels that her husband no longer loves her, what do you do? The option of slyly revealing the presence of a "secret" but not identifying its content seems too gamey to be of much real value.

The real point here is that the guides you elect to operate by are important. When I receive a telephone call, letter, etc., it's my policy to lead off the next meeting with a full disclosure. This at least clears the air and keeps us on track. Of course, it also keeps me from being tied up and worried about needing to keep a secret. One of my favorite cartoons depicts a therapist sitting in a chair bound and gagged. The client is saying, "Doctor, I'm in such pain. Why won't you help me?" While this may be inevitable from time to time, let's at least not supply the rope and gag.

There's one additional element to consider here. Since one of my beliefs is that anxiety is needed to fuel change, I'm not interested in prematurely reducing their tension. To do so would be countertherapeutic. Accepting secrets often has a confessional type effect. That is, it lessens the guilt but unfortunately also diminishes their motivation to change.

My view of families is that the members are massively inter-connected. I have very little confidence in the notion that ideas or information can lead to growth. In order for real change to occur, the family needs to engage each other emotionally. They need real experiences, not cerebral insights. My style is to emphasize emotional experiences, not educational learnings.

The goal of therapy is to help families reach a more adaptive, fulfilling level of living. Mere symptom remission is not enough. I see symptom remission as a side effect of productive therapy, not as the goal of it. In fact, it may be that symptom-free living is merely a destructive delusion. A more realistic and enjoyable goal would be to develop the freedom to have a family life that encourages rotating scapegoats. All family members could then benefit from the experience of playing all the positions.

3
Process of Family Therapy: Political/Administrative Aspects and Stages of Therapy

The journey of family therapy begins with a blind date and ends with the empty nest. As with any other kind of relationship, it passes through a number of phases and struggles along the way. While many of the issues are predictable, the outcome is always in doubt. You don't really know if you're going to make it with a new person.

When you answer the telephone and are asked out by a perfect, or not so perfect, stranger, a complicated sequence of sizing up and testing out typically commences. In addition to finding out how your name and number were discovered, you quickly broach the topics of mutual acquaintances, overlapping interests and specific plans for the date. If this were to follow the old-fashioned scenario, the woman being asked out would rather carefully size up the prospective suitor and his intentions. If his proposal included a late meeting in a secluded place, she might counter with her own suggestion. Perhaps lunch with three of her best friends at the most public place in town would be her offer. He would then be free to take it or leave it. In any event, she would feel that she had acted wisely.

When initially sought out by a family, the therapist is in a similar dilemma. Do you accept without question the proposal they are making? Do you engage in some give and take to be sure the relationship starts off on acceptable terms? It's my conviction that the therapist must always start off by identifying the proposal of the family, then make any counterproposal he deems fit to get the ball rolling. In fact, I think it's typically advisable to make some kind of counterdemand right off the bat. You need to protect yourself from just being coopted by the family. While there's no need to rigidly dictate an impossible series of conditions, you do need to take a clear position. A two-way political process ensues. This initial appointment-setting

telephone exchange sets the tone for what is to follow. This
initial struggle is called the Battle for Structure.

Battle for Structure

The key point here is for the therapist to face the need to act
with personal and professional integrity. You must act on what
you believe. Betrayals help no one. The Battle for Structure is
really you coming to grips with yourself and then presenting
this to them. It's not a technique or a power play. It's a setting of
the minimum conditions you require before beginning.

Mom: Hello, Dr. Whitaker? I'm Mrs. Johnson and would like
to talk with you regarding some problems I'm having.
My family physician, Dr. Jones, gave me your name.

Carl: Sure. Get your husband and we can set up a time.

Mom: Well, that's not what I had in mind. You see he's a very
busy man. Besides, he doesn't really believe in talking
about problems.

Carl: It looks like we've got a problem. You see I don't work
with individuals.

Mom: Well, wouldn't you see me alone just this first time? That
way I could explain the full situation to you.

Carl: No, I'm sorry. I couldn't do that.

Mom: But I haven't really told him I was calling you. It might
upset him.

Carl: Sorry.

Mom: But Dr. Jones said you could help me. He specifically
gave me your name. Now you're saying that you won't
help me?

Carl: No, I'm not saying that.

Mom: Then you will see me without my husband?

Carl: No . . . but if you bring him along we could meet.

Mom: Well . . . I'll try. But I can't make any promises.

Carl: That's fine. Neither can I. When you get it organized, we can meet. By the way, it would also be important to bring the kids in.

Mom: Now that would really be a mistake. They don't know that Jack and I are having a hard time. We don't want to expose them to too much.

Carl: I see them as being important in the family too. It's really necessary that they be here.

Mom: I couldn't possibly do that.

Carl: Well, I respect your right to make that choice.

Mom: So you'll see us without the kids?

Carl: No, I didn't say that.

Mom: OK. OK. What time do you have free?

Having struggled through this opening snag, therapy has a chance to begin on a productive note. The most poignant discovery I've made in doing this type of telephone struggle is that the outcome has more to do with me than with them. They sense how convinced I am about what I'm saying and respond accordingly.

If you believe you need a certain grouping before it's worth your time or their energy to begin, you'll get it. It's not a matter of bullying them. It's an issue of your letting them know what's important to you. Of course, until you know what you believe, it's hard to be clear. But beware, excessive flexibility pays off only for contortionists. You can get two generations, three generations, sometimes four if you ask. Boyfriends, girlfriends, ex-spouses, current lovers, etc. are all game if you approach it.

I remember one session attended by an attorney and his wife, ex-wife, and current girlfriend. It was wild listening to the three women comparing notes on him for two hours. He was glad to get back to the courtroom.

The Battle for Structure is the period of initial political jousting with the family. I need to establish what Bowen would call an "I position" in relation to the family. As they begin to hear and absorb the conditions and limitations I am presenting, their automatic response is to begin to piece together their own "we position." While it typically takes time to fully develop, the initiation of this sort of unifying process is one of the core aspects of working with families. It is a step in the evolution of a sense of family loyalty or nationalism. At some level, all families do have a sense of loyalty waiting to be called forth. The more clear emergence of their sense of family identification and pride is not something that needs to be created; the seeds are already there. It needs only the opportunity to take root and grow.

There are at least two levels to attend to in considering these conditions for therapy. One deals with the reality, factual component — who attends the sessions, who is asked to talk first, what the therapist accepts as a definition of the problem, etc. These decisions are always made (even deciding not to decide is a decision) and merit direct attention by the therapist. Your actual decisions may vary from time to time. They certainly would be expected to vary from therapist to therapist. My own thinking concerning these matters has crystallized over time but remains variable to some extent. These variations tend to reflect my own processes at a deeper level. My beliefs and values dictate what is negotiable and what isn't.

In setting these conditions, I want to engage the family in an interactive process that leads to an experiential exchange. In order for the process of therapy to be impactful rather than merely educational or social, it must consist of real experiences, not just head trips. While education may seem useful, it typically leads only to a more sophisticated way of explaining life, not living it.

The other crucial component in this process is the capacity of the therapist to take seriously his own needs. Becoming a professional martyr by sacrificing yourself to the family is hardly an appropriate model. Giving up or compromising your own beliefs, standards and needs leads only to therapist burnout. I'm convinced burnout is a side effect of our own failed integrity struggle, not a function of our struggle with them. Your decision to try to turn into what you think they want is your fault.

My standard comment to families of "I'm not really here for you. I'm here for what I can get out of it" is one way of saying I'm not really for hire as a professional prostitute. It lets them know that I will remain the center of my own living. That they need not worry about protecting me. Again, real caring requires distance (caring for self) and the capacity to get personally involved. Unless the core impetus for you is your growth, it degenerates into "helping." Once this occurs all is lost. They become inept and you impotent.

This remark also reflects my belief that if I can get something personal out of my contact with the family, the experience between us will be alive. The aliveness of the experience then also affords them the opportunity to grow. I want to create the conditions where growth is possible, but fully accept that I can't force or orchestrate it.

Joining

The idea of joining is important to consider here. Joining is the process of developing enough of a connection to at least feel that continuing on is worth pursuing. While we often think of it as something the therapist does to a family, I've come to see it as something we do with a family. That is, we engage in some kind of an experience with each other.

The quality of that experience comes from a number of factors. Part of it is the undercurrent sense of how willing we are to get involved with each other. Does the family sense that we have the capacity or even want to get to know them and understand them? Can we really listen? Can we respond in a real, rather than phoney way? Do we sense they are people we're willing to invest in? The personal criteria are endless.

Another factor is the automatic joining that emerges out of a common background, similar experiences, or shared perspectives. This kind of shared essence connotes an increased capacity for empathy. We're not as dependent on mere words to convey the depth of our experience. Of course, this level of connection also carries the built-in dilemma of blind spots and overidentification. I "know" what he means when a farm father talks about being an isolate, or loving the cows. Unfortunately, I may have no sense that there's anything problematic about it. But at least I can get in there.

With this sort of too familiar family, I must also work to discover ways to step away from them and gain some distance. I might play with toys in an absentminded fashion, take pages of notes to be visually distracted, or work with a cotherapist so I have a "we" to belong to.

Establish a Metaposition

In beginning, my effort is to establish a metaposition in relation to the family. I want them to understand more of what they can expect from me and what I expect from them. This is not designed as a relationship between peers. I want it understood that in my role as a therapist I'm a member of an older generation.

The metaphor of a coach of a baseball team is a good way of describing what the relationship will be. As the coach, I'm really not interested in playing on the team, only in helping them play more effectively. If I allow myself to be seduced into playing first base for them, it will be difficult to return to the metaposition of a coach. They will rightfully expect me to actually make the plays for them.

The more destructive message it gives, however, is that I don't think much of the first baseman they already have. It's a way of saying to them that my way of living is better than theirs. It's a tricky way of trying to convince them to give up on developing their own resources and to buy my brand instead. That kind of sabotage they can do without.

Convening the Clan

One of my ways of concretizing this issue is to try to convene the full clan before starting. Just as it would be foolish for a coach to begin the game without fielding a full team, there is considerable risk in commencing therapy without all the key characters present. The missing members may feel discounted in that they are not considered vital to the overall family functioning. They also typically develop a justifiable sense of paranoia regarding what was said in their absence. When either of these reactions is pronounced, the seeds of sabotage take root. I want the permission of the entire unit to get involved. A concerted effort by any absent family member to undermine the capacity of the family to change typically succeeds.

This guideline of convening the clan represents an effort to create a sense of the family as a unit and to validate the value of each individual member. It also serves to avoid a powerful source of sabotage and forces them to capitulate to my belief that the whole family is the patient. Finally, it minimizes the likelihood that I will be drawn into a position of destructive overinvolvement.

A side effect of this decision is that, with the full family present, there is a clear escalation in their level of anxiety. With everyone there, there is no one to talk about behind the back, no one to blame without interpersonal repercussions, and no way to deny what was discussed. This type of anxiety typically makes change more possible.

It seems particularly dangerous to decide to hold the session when the wife-mother or husband-father is absent. For example, meeting without the husband-father is a clear way of auditioning for the part. You're meeting with people already involved in relationships. Therefore, involving yourself in the wife-husband dyad by standing in for him automatically creates a triangle. The kids, too, may see you as a preferable father. This is a strange position for someone interested in being useful to a family, unless of course you're unhappy with your own.

The theoretical notion of an emergent property also enters here. The notion of an emergent property states that you can't really get a sense of an organism by dissecting and examining the component parts. While you can generate ideas and develop hypotheses about the full family based on contact with part of it, the error or distortion factor is unnecessarily elevated. By definition, the level of inference involved is escalated. It brings to mind the story of the three blind men who tried to describe an elephant based on touching only one of the parts. The different perspectives provided by the trunk, ear and leg are profound. So it is with families.

Perhaps the most disastrous effect of this, though, is what happens to the family. Meeting with less than the full group deprives them of the opportunity for the optimal therapeutic experience. Rather than unifying the family, triangles, alliances and coalitions are formed.

Beginning with Dad

Early in the initial session there are some additional avenues I pursue. It's my normal style to really commence the interview by asking the father to tell me how the family really works. This follows directly from my belief that men are much less emotionally involved and available than are women. If Dad can be prodded to come alive emotionally and become a real human being, it may offer unexpected hope to the entire family. Rather than allowing Dad to act like he's the guy who lives next door, I want him to move in.

Carl: So, Dad, could you tell me something about the family?

Dad: Sure. We decided to call you because of a problem we're having with our daughter. She's been skipping too much school and it just has to stop.

Carl: That's what your wife said over the phone. She told me a little about that.

Right now I'm more interested in hearing something about the family and how it operates.

Dad: I'm not sure what you mean.

Carl: If I had asked you to tell me about the Green Bay Packers football team, you'd know what to say. You know, who produces, who doesn't. How well the quarterback and receivers work together. Who is the spiritual/emotional leader.

I assume you know more about your family than about the Packers.

Dad: I'm still not sure what you want to hear.

Carl: Well, maybe you could start with something about you. You know, what your concerns are. The things you lie awake worrying about at night. What your most personal fears are. Anything that would get us started.

This way of beginning is really more complicated than merely focusing first on Dad. It's really about pulling in and engaging the emotional outsiders. By getting them involved, the configuration changes. New potentials are opened. It's standard for me to leave Mom and any identified patients for the end. I want to talk with all of the other family members before turning to them.

Expand the Symptoms

The preceding vignette also touches on another early maneuver. Families typically come to therapy with one particular family member manifesting a symptom that has the family concerned. My perspective is that this really should be viewed as a ticket for entry. Never believe the story that this is the only, or even the most significant, issue in the family. My goal is to as quickly as possible expand the picture of what the problems are and why they're here.

It's like beginning a game of poker. It's important for everyone to ante up. Some families do this with relative ease, while others are thoroughly resistant to the very notion. The resistive families are actually more frightened than resistant and it is often stimulating to challenge them in this regard.

Recently, a family of three — mother, father and six-year-old daughter — attended an initial session. The daughter was considered school phobic. Mother was quite obese and Father was obviously a hard-driving, type A career man. My initial efforts to expand the family symptom beyond Sarah's school fears were unsuccessful. Dad played dumb, refusing to address any personal concerns and denying any relationship struggles. Mom came to his aid when I pressed about his overdedication to his career. She commented on how proud she was of her husband and his career success. In only a few years he had risen to a powerful position within a respected firm. Even though he worked nearly 75 hours a week and was frequently out late, she had accepted this as the price of success. She closed her statement by adding that her husband was the kind of man who really needed to be immersed in a fast-paced, exciting business world. The following exchange then followed.

Carl: You mean he's totally lost interest in you?

Mom: Well, no, it's not that. It's just that his way of contributing to the family is to make sure that we have everything we need.

Carl: Except a husband and father you mean.

Mom: No. He's a good father.

Carl: (*turning to the daughter*) Sarah, do you think that Mommy worries that Daddy might be kissing his secretary?
You know he's gone at work so much. Maybe he gets lonely too.

Sar: No. Daddies don't get lonely. Just Mommies, but since Mommy has me, she doesn't have to be lonely either.

Carl: Well, I'm sure glad you take such good care of your Mommy but I still worry about Daddies. It's very hard to tell when they're lonely.

Having laid the groundwork for them to begin to wonder about their relationship, while not pushing for an overt exploration at that moment, I continued the session in a different direction. They naturally returned to the issue of Sarah's refusal to go to school. We danced around the obvious issue of her dedication to Mom and her desire to help Mom hide from her sense of depression.

Later in the same session, I wanted Mom to have the opportunity to really take a look at herself. She was complaining of her inability to play tennis with her high-powered husband because of her weight.

Carl: (*turning to Dad*) Do you worry about her weight, too, or do you prefer playing with other partners?

Dad: Of course I'd love to have her pick up the sport, but it's just not possible. It would be dangerous for her to exert herself with so much excess weight.

Carl: So you don't want to feel like you killed her by pushing
     tennis. I suppose I can understand that.
         How is it that you manage to live with the knowledge
     that she's slowly committing suicide via her obesity?

The symptom framework has now been expanded. Extra-
marital affairs, self-destructive overeating, and a relationship
gap have been set forth. While they may not really agree with
some of these formulations, they leave the session with more to
consider. It's not really necessary that they agree. My job was
to complicate their initial oversimplification that distorted the
family reality.

In addition to merely broadening the symptom constellation, I also strive to change their perspective to an interpersonal viewpoint. When Sarah's school refusal is attached to a
protective function with her mother, the picture shifts. It begins to focus on a family issue, not on individual quirks or
pathology. By involving Dad in Mom's overeating, I make this
a relationship function, not an indication of lack of willpower.

Another aspect of this work centers on the capacity of the
therapist to be "mean." In this context, "meanness" represents
both a willingness to be honest in my reaction to them and a
refusal to sell out by being artificially nurturing. It's my responsibility to help them take a more courageous look at themselves. Covering up concerns and ignoring problem areas are
of no value to anyone. They can get that at home.

In striving to be as honest as I can, my goal is to trigger a
real interaction that is not restricted to mere social role-play-
ing. I want it to be more personal. When viewed from this
perspective, the more traditional posture of automatic caring
can be seen only as being painfully superficial. In order for
caring to be real, it must be embedded in a context that is
honest. In a backwards kind of way, my "meanness" is a representation of my capacity to care.

By this time the family has been exposed to some of my way
of thinking. Another phase of therapy comes to the front. This

is called the Battle for Initiative. In this phase, the issue is to push the family to be more proactive. They need to assume more responsibility for what transpires in the therapy.

Battle for Initiative

When you have successfully struggled through the Battle for Structure by establishing your metaposition and conditions for therapy, the process shifts. Now that the family has, in a sense, capitulated to your demands, the risk is that they'll go flat and leave the ball in your court. The next phase, then, is to get them to take responsibility for what happens in therapy. The undercurrent feeling is sometimes, "OK, Whitaker, you've made us play your way. If you think you're so hot, you fix us." This is dangerous territory. Some may find it appealing to their narcissism, I find it scary and absurd.

It's not unusual for the second interview to begin something like this.

Dad: Well, what should we talk about?

Carl: I'm not really sure.

Dad: Do you have any more questions to ask us? Do you need to know any more information?

Carl: No. No thanks. I feel comfortable like this.

(*silence*)

Mom: Do you think we should continue where we left off last time, or would you prefer that we move to a new topic?

Carl: It's fine with me either way.

(*silence*)

Dad: Well, I for one would like a little direction. After all, we're paying you for your expertise, not just to sit there.

Carl: I'm not really interested in telling you what's important for you to talk about. You know yourself better than I do.

My expertise tells me that what I think isn't very important right now. What you choose to do with each other is what's crucial.

Dad: What value are you to us then? Why do we need you?

Carl: I'm not sure that you do. I'm here to try to augment your effort to be more alive with each other.

It would be flat-out stupid of me to try to tell you how to live. My patterns of living are no more valid than yours. You need to get the game started.

At this point in the therapy, the struggle is to get them to take over. To have the courage to take the initiative to face themselves and not look to the therapist to do it for them. You need to disrupt the fantasy that you'll make it all better.

It's often a period accented by tension and anxious silences. I look at it as the water heating up in the coffeepot before it can percolate. It's not a matter of the therapist being a nobody. It's an issue of the family becoming a somebody. They need to grapple with each other. It's an invitation to them to come alive and stop play-acting.

The issue of their looking to me for a solution, much like the idea that if someone gave you the "magic words" you'd have it made, can be damaging to the family. When they consciously place the possibility of change directly in my hands, they're undermining themselves. I want them to face the reality that they're the real players, but I offer the comfort that I'm a competent coach.

It's imperative that this learning come about via some sort of experiential exchange, not via detached teaching. Another way I try to impart this idea is to never initiate talk about having another session. They need to broach that topic. They need to jointly decide if they're going to return. If they don't address it, neither do I. I often push it the other way by refusing to set another appointment until they go home and talk about it.

Therapeutic Alliance

The successful completion of the Battle for Structure and the Battle for Initiative forms what I think of as a therapeutic alliance. Only when we've established the nature of our relationship and they've taken the reins are we ready to go forward. We're now a functional suprasystem.

The whole idea of forming a therapeutic alliance with a family is tricky. My intent is to identify the family as the patient. I'm not interested in accepting the black sheep they offer, or the white knight they revere (Be careful! The white knight is every bit as vulnerable as the black sheep), or even a subsystem as a valid patient. I'm not even willing to accept them all as patients in serial order. It's the family I make my deal with. The family transcends the sum of the parts.

It's my capacity to always see them as one multifaceted organism, massively interconnected, that permits my alliance with them. While it may not be detectable to an observer, it's been my experience that the family can sense that I'm interested in them as a unit.

This evolves into a phase where the politics become less central. Our connection takes on more of a personal quality. As we're released from this struggle, there is more freedom to be spontaneous and creative. I'm able to access more and more of my internal associations and images. I'm free to be responsive *to* them rather than responsible *for* them. Typically, the family is more accepting of my moves to get more personal, as well as my decisions to separate or move out. I can individuate and belong without too much distortion. They're clearly less dependent and have a better sense of themselves. Our increasing comfort with individuating and joining reflects real growth and marks a more adaptive, healthy system.

It's during this period that the family begins to make some

changes. They move forward and are able to risk more without the shield of their presenting problem. Each step they take is important and I want to make sure they realize they did the changing, not me. I try to encourage their movement without directing it.

We might compare experiences, share dreams, etc. My associations become more vivid. For example, when talking with a family about the way Dad's anger immediately made everyone go flat, an image popped into my head. "You know, I just had the craziest idea. Do you ever have them, too? The image was that of a giant-sized Cuisinart-type thing labeled 'people grinder.' I assume its function was to do to Dad what his anger just did to all of you. Are you planning to get one?"

This led to a much more direct discussion of their fear of Dad. Eventually, it wound around to Dad not liking the ogre role, but not knowing how to be anything else.

Termination

As the family growth continues, they use more and more of their own resources. They develop the confidence to reject my thinking and begin to more deeply trust their own. They see me as more and more human, with frailties now included. They are free to tease me regarding mistakes or stupid ideas. In effect, they begin to see me as a person, not just a role. They become their own therapist. They assume responsibility for their own living.

Regardless of my sense of impending loss, it's my job to send them off with my blessings. Much like any parent feels when the children leave for college, I experience a sense of loss. But I give them my blessing and they're free to return any time they choose. They don't leave empty-handed though. The impact of the shared therapy experience is interwoven into their life tapestry.

The decision to leave must remain theirs. It's their life. If things have gone well, they leave with more lovingness and more freedom to be real people.

As I sense this phase approaching, I even listen for hints or clues that suggest their readiness to leave. When I detect them, I make them overt. The decision to terminate must be handled with care. It is countertherapeutic to try to interfere with their decision to leave. You must respect their process.

Empty Nest

The new coffee mug that reads, "Life's a bitch. Then you die," sometimes seems appropriate. When the family goes off, there is a sense of loss. We've invested in each other and now experience the pain of separation. While there is often a joyful side, the loss is real.

Since this is such a common part of the life of a therapist, some precautions are in order. Having a professional cuddle group is the best way to ease the pain. When you belong to a group, you're never really alone. It's best to not insist that your family take care of all of these needs. The capacity to separate your professional role from your real life living is essential.

Additional Issues

Establishing the Menu

One of the really exciting aspects of an initial session is that since it's a blind date, no one really knows each other. This allows you to poke and probe around without the sense of it being premeditated. I typically make it a point to venture into a wide range of difficult topics during that first meeting. It's a magic moment of sorts. Families can handle probes about almost anything without clamming up. When you establish these issues as being relevant to living, there is a tacit agreement that we can return to them later. The topics of murderousness, suicidal impulses, sexual impulses, etc. all merit mention.

When these primitive issues are established as being normal, they become less toxic.

If you fail to do this early on, you will later encounter more denial and defensiveness. When you ask about Mom's homicidal impulses in the tenth session, she suspects you're asking because of something you see in her, not just because you know that all people have such impulses.

Dealing with Impasses

Impasses are inevitable! Periods where you feel stuck and don't know which way to turn are just part of the process.

My favorite way to break through this kind of place is to invite a consultant into the next session. This gives me someone to be united with. It offers binocular vision and gives me space to see things differently. In addition to helping me, a consultant helps the family by ruining their magical fantasy that only I could help them. As they now more clearly see some of my self-doubt, they face the issue of the need to change.

The fresh viewpoint of a consultant often breaks logjams and helps pull the therapist out of a coopted position. Sometimes a real shake-up is in order.

4
Symbolic-Experiential
Family Therapy

The whole business of symbolic therapy is difficult to talk about in a non-symbolic way. It's like talking about love. You can find words to represent only a rather surface level of it. Talking in metaphor, as the poets have discovered, may offer the only hope.

I've come to look at symbolic therapy as being similar to the infrastructure of a city. It's looking at the stuff that runs underneath the streets and buildings that is important. This is what permits life on the surface to go on. Even though I may not see them, when I look outside I know there are gas lines and water lines, sometimes telephone lines, lying beneath the surface. This subterranean world is essential to what goes on everywhere. In addition to its not being directly observable, another characteristic of this level of operations is that it has a broad, general sort of impact on a whole variety of homes, offices and businesses. The effect is pervasive.

This is similar to how I conceptualize symbolic therapy. Our personal subterranean worlds are dominated by the flow of impulses and evolving symbols. While they are not always visible, I know they're there. I don't have to wonder about it or question it. Just as water flows through pipes under our streets, impulses flow through our unconscious. We're all the same in that way. We all have these emotional infrastructures that insure the flow of our impulse life. While often hidden from view, or at least disguised, they exist.

It's hard to really look at family therapy without seeing it as a symbolic parenting project of the highest order. After all, the family comes to us with the idea that we can help them, we can make them better. We, of course, wouldn't be in this crazy racket if we weren't, to some degree, afflicted with the same notion. We want to be helpful to others, to lead them to fuller

73

and happier lives. We want to lessen some of the suffering in the world.

The catch comes in when we move from this idea to operationalizing what it means we have to do. How do we manage to assist, or be helpful in, the family's growth effort without unwittingly undermining the very progress sought? Again, it's the issue of whether we view ourselves as real parents, with all the attendant obligations of seeing to it that our children do the right things, or are we less concretely obligated? Can we afford to leave the reality dimension of choice and action up to them? Maybe the real question is: Can we afford not to?

It's clear enough in my mind that the therapist must occupy a metaposition in relation to the family. That is, you must keep an overview of the full group, maintain some distance, and not be sucked into taking over at the reality level. While I'm intensely interested in talking with them about their living and participating in a real experience in the therapy room, it stops there. I have no real interest in being central in their decision-making process in real life. They must retain control at this level and it's up to me to see to it that they do so. Not only do I need to avoid taking over, but I need to prevent them from seeing me as someone who even could. The concrete events of their living are of interest only because they are manifestations of their emotional and relational understructures, not because of their literal reality.

It's really an interesting juxtaposition. I enter the relationship unwilling to be seduced into being too literal and reality-oriented. The family comes in thinking they want concretes. They want me to offer them solutions for their living, to provide them with the magic potion that will take away their ills. Even the physician in me knows that's ridiculous. I often respond to this kind of request by telling them that my magic wand has been out of order ever since a curious little 4-year-old pulled the star off the stick, turning it into a deadly Chinese star. There are no magic words, gimmicks or communications exercises that will transform them into a perpetually euphoric group. Life involves struggle and relationships take work. There are no ways to avoid this.

But it's not hopeless! People can learn to live more productive and intimate lives. They can find increasing levels of satisfaction and joy. The key lies in their capacity to experience the world in a broader and deeper manner. As our experience of living expands, we live richer lives, even when the reality elements remain unchanged.

Of course, reality situations do sometimes change, too. It's not that I'm opposed to real world change. Far from it! It's just that the role I carve out for myself is not really focused on the reality events of their living. I don't live in the fantasy that I'm in charge of their reality. As we interact in the symbolic/experiential world, however, they may extract something that will lead them to change their living. I don't change them, but often they do change.

Symbol World

We all filter our experience of living through a relatively narrow number of constructs. It's the richness or poverty of these constructs that goes a long way in determining the subjective experience of living. Like the Eskimo's capacity to experience 17 different kinds of snow, as opposed to the single category of snow known to the sunbelt urbanite. The meaning and impact of external reality are determined by our internal reality. The same symphony can be experienced as being glorifyingly stimulating or painfully boring. It depends on the ear of the listener.

In a growth-oriented therapy, the central issue is to focus on expanding the significance of experience and broadening the horizons of life. We organize our lives around our own limited, internal representational systems. The richer and more diverse this world, the more freedom and creativity we have. If we can aid in the expansion of the symbolic world of the families we see, they can live richer lives.

There are a number of universal issues that, by virtue of our being human, we are blessed, as well as cursed, to grapple with. Issues such as loneliness, rage, sexuality, and death are part of all of us. We all carry homicidal, suicidal, and primitive sexual impulses. It's part of the human condition. Much of our internal living then touches on these issues, while much of what we show externally is designed to be more socially tolerable. Our culture prohibits the primitive expression of these impulses, forcing us to keep them in check. Despite these social injunctions, they continue to be profoundly active internally. These impulses leave their mark on much, if not all, of our concrete living. At the undercurrent level of primitive impulses, life is timeless. Past, present and future are merged.

In addition to being pervasive, the world of impulses and symbols is multileveled. Symbols range from absolute universals to being wholly idiographic. Direct representations of our basic impulse life are universally available. These primary impulses find similar expression in all cultures. The sexual symbols, the baring of teeth in anger, the despairing look of loneliness, or the terror of facing death are familiar to all peoples. Each culture may also leave a particular imprint on the representational world of its people. While the oedipal theme cuts across cultures, there are literally dozens of cultural variations. Each culture may also develop its own way of expressing friendship, celebrating birth, marking adolescence, and grieving death.

Each area of the symbol world must also be more personally defined within the mythology of each family. Thus, the universal survival instinct, as glorified in this culture by the myth of the self-made man, receives a more idiographic face when interpreted by any particular family. "We're the Smiths. Being a Smith means you never ask for a handout. We carry our own weight" is one typical interpretation of the universal instinct. The specific way this perspective is applied will powerfully influence each family member.

In some families, the core survival instinct we began with

may end up distorted into an intense, relentless need to achieve . . . a workaholic interpretation. They may pursue "success" at the expense of relationships, ending up with the bank full and their personal lives empty. Others may seek a more balanced life, but remain conflicted by guilt over their relative lack of tangible success. The variations are endless.

The way any particular family enacts their symbol world may evolve over time, but typically retains some core manifestations that are more or less consistent. One way to catch a glimpse of their core model is to look at their interpersonal family rituals. Attending to how they operate when physically together is revealing. The morning routine, the dinner time ritual, and how they function during holidays are undertakings that tell how their world is organized.

How does the father fit the culture's image of strength, the mother of nurturance? How are masculinity and femininity defined and expressed? Does the group retain too much power over the individuals or not enough? How do they negotiate individuation and belonging? How are the holidays dealt with? The family's symbolic representational system is on display here. These events tend to show what the family is.

Looking Within

There's really only one way to "understand" the complex world of impulses and symbols. That way is to look within. Only when you can really identify a certain basic impulse within yourself do you really know that it exists. Once you've discovered it in yourself, it becomes real. Until then, it remains merely a nice concept or theory, but is of little value to you. I believe the formula works the other way, too. If you can't find it within you, then for all practical purposes it doesn't exist. If you've never been able to identify and face your own homicidal impulses, you really won't be able to believe they exist. Not in "normal" people anyway. By definition, then, anyone who admits to such impulses is abnormal according to your covert internal norms.

My beliefs go the other way. I believe part of the human condition is to have within you a rich and bubbling impulse life. We're all murderous, we all struggle with suicidal impulses, we all have incestuous fantasies, we're all terrified by the notion of death. To fail to face these simple facts of life is to seal off much of your humanness.

Your own awareness of your impulse world is really a prerequisite to your capacity to see, let alone understand, the symbol world of others. To the extent that you can face the multiple symbolic manifestations of your own impulses, you are free to generalize this capacity to your dealings with others.

Symbolic-Experiential Therapy

The whole idea of symbolic-experiential therapy emerges from the fact that while we think about and talk about things on one level, we live on a level that's a very different territory. Symbolic therapy, then, is involved in the effort to move directly into the level of living, not settling for the realm of thinking, talking or reasoning. It's a therapy where you're not dealing with the data the family presents as data. It's not education. The old saying, "Nothing worth knowing can be taught" comes to mind. It's not social adaptation training. Symbolic therapy is an effort to deal with the representation system underneath what's actually being said. It involves picking up on the symbolic bits and fragments that you detect or sense. Each of these bits represents another territory, an infrastructure that runs beneath our surface living.

I think of it as an attempt to push into a more holistic territory of living, not to remain trapped in the thinking territory. It's an extrapolation of sorts from the old Gestalt pattern that included body motion, body sensation, and a more total awareness. I see that as part of a gradual evolution away from the

Freudian intrapsychic set to a pattern of interpersonal therapy and an interactive worldview.

Symbolic therapy centers around the notion that there are a number of universal issues in life. Issues that are so loaded that we often deal with them only in disguised or hidden ways. While they may be too frightening to face at the surface level, they do permeate the understructure level of our living.

Symbolic therapy, therefore, focuses on helping people become more comfortable in their impulse living, to be less frightened by it, and to integrate it more fully into their concrete living. The impulse world is not one to be avoided. You can't escape it!

The only way to honestly encourage people to venture forth into such frightening territory is to use yourself. The therapist must be willing to expose some of his own symbolic experiences. To reveal his personal belief system. To offer glimpses into his infrastructure. When you dare to expose the family to this, in tiny fragments, they're left with slivers of you in them. When they come face to face with part of your insides, they have to decide what to do with it. They're free to produce their own extrapolations, depending on how it reverberates inside of them.

If the therapist, for example, starts talking about himself as an imperfect being, or reveals his feelings of dependency, fear, or confusion, the family may be tempted to look inwards too. This approach is geared to offering them a mirror-image opportunity of exploring and maybe exposing more of their own belief system, of their infrastructure. Making personal the femininity in men, the masculinity in women, or the infantilization we all feel can lead to growth. All of these territories can be opened up. They are areas people don't ordinarily talk about, or even think about, probably because they are too important.

One of the exciting aspects of this sort of work is the discovery that as the therapy evolves and we are more and more free to engage in a symbolic exchange, it becomes a growth experience for me too. Often it seems that the more I get out of it, the more they get out of it. The outcome of a meeting of our symbol worlds can be truly exciting. In a sense, we all become patients to the process.

One of the classic patterns of symbolic therapy is the process of dealing with death. The death of the therapist, the death of a family member, the universal fact of death and that no one is spared. All of these areas can be profound in their impact. We all wish to be able to freeze time, to live forever, and to be eternally remembered. In a culture that carefully struggles to depersonalize death and automatically wriggles to deny it, the experience of facing it with open eyes can be profound. The idea that it's only by facing your own personal death that you're free to really live is hauntingly accurate.

In a similar vein, the topics of "craziness," suicide, homicide, sexuality, etc. all carry considerable weight. For example, I frequently say to family members, "If you were to really go crazy, you know, really flip out, how would you do it? Take a rifle up to the tower for some target practice on the people below? Run away to the woods to become a tree? What would your own personal craziness really look like?" By doing this, I'm encouraging the external expression of their internal life in a nondestructive manner. It's an opportunity to look at your own impulse world without the fear that it will really take over. By facing them, you can begin to integrate the impulses rather than preserve them intact via isolation. Efforts to isolate and deny impulses typically intensify them, often to the point that when they do gain expression, it's more apt to be undercontrolled and explosive.

My probing and prodding do not require that the full impulse load come out all at once. It's often preferable to have it emerge in smaller bits. For example, asking a new bride to share her homicidal impulses regarding her husband may be too unnerving. However, asking if she had ever considered oversalting his food as a way of getting even with him or even rid of him is more tolerable.

To help them break new ground, I might share some of my

associations or press them to entertain the polar opposites of their opening positions. For example, of the husband who proclaims to love his wife so much that he'd die if she rejected him, I might ask, "Have you settled on homicide as the only way to break the tyranny?" To the wife who claims to love her husband too much to ever criticize him, I might reply, "That's absolutely vicious."

In these examples, I want to break the set of love being the opposite of hate. I want them presented as yoked feelings. If you've got one, the other is automatically present. When the artificial dichotomizing of these emotions is removed, the framework for more honesty is set. With enough struggle, this may even lead to intimacy. I want to push them into a new territory, one where their old level of living, and thinking about living, no longer suffices. By experiencing contamination by way of my belief system, they may be freed to experience more of their own impulse world, thereby becoming more human.

I'll often try to expand the family's understanding of symptoms by extending them backwards through the previous generations. Another method is to propel them forward into the next generation. By assuming that symptoms have a continuity through the generations, I want to help them access the rich symbol world that runs through the extended family. If there are 10 children in the family, I want them to know that the way the next generation deals with family size is clearly connected to the present family experience. They may strive to match the 10 or adamantly refuse to have any children. The modeling can be positive or negative. Most typically, it contains bits of both. In a similar fashion, the family myths of parenthood, spousal life, etc. are all richly intertwined.

Encouraging them to be less oppressively heavy with each other can also facilitate growth. I often tease about role flexibility within the family. By asking Dad when was the last time he felt secure enough to allow 6-year-old Mikey to pour the milk, or lead the prayers, or decide what television programs the family would watch, the notion of change is introduced. It works the other way too. Maybe Dad could learn to curl up and talk baby talk as the four- and five-year-old kids played parents. These kinds of role reversals can have a freeing impact on all family members.

Confusion

One of the basic tenets behind symbolic work is to help people expand their range of life experience. To open them to a broader range of living. Being able to break their set typically requires a real contamination of their current perspective . . . a deprogramming experience. One of the most powerful ways to do this is through the power of confusion. I want to be able to disrupt their certainties and destroy their notion that life is simple. When the neatness of their right/wrong dichotomy is eliminated, a new world opens up. They are then faced with the growth issues of choice, values and responsibility in an uncertain world. Again, I want to participate in an experience that shakes them. One that surprises them enough to break free of the family-of-origin hypnosis we all are subject to.

Confusion is, by itself, one of the most potent ways of symbolically opening up the infrastructure of the family. Whenever a family member says something, I want to be able to be useful by revising or modifying or twisting it in such a way that they are not left with an empty statement. I want them left with new options and considerations to explore. This leaves them with the possibility of exploring new territories, while at worst leaving them with a contamination that, because of its universality, can't be easily dismissed.

To a childishly demanding husband, the comment, "I miss my mommy too," can have a significant impact. Even if it's never again mentioned, there can be a significant result. I've also not given him anything specific to really disagree with me about. This leaves him stuck with the message.

One of the best ways to offer a family the benefit of confusion is for the therapist to freely make use of the universal beliefs he has about people and families. By deliberately focusing on the fact that all families share certain commonalities, you are free to move with less inhibition. By assuming that all the stress, all the health, all the pathology in any one family are also available and operative in every other family, you are ready to dance with them. While some of these areas may be under cover and hidden from awareness, they still exist.

The capacity of the therapist to operate from such a base of universals, even though they're not yet apparent in this particular family, is crucial. It allows you to operate at a level of inference. While they remain loyal to the "facts" of their consciousness, you can operate on a different plane. This allows you to move directly to the infrastructure level, while they remain constrained by their reality. This discontinuity can then generate confusion. More specifically, any part of the psychotherapy process that can be directly subsumed under the family's ordinary, programmed thought process is not growthful or useful. Confusion is the real essence of unlearning and new learning. If there is no confusion, there can be no change, no progress. Until you break with your patterns, the ruts continue to deepen. Life goes on, as living dies.

One of the major concerns that haunts anyone who works with families is how to have an impact that means anything. How to be involved in a way that actually makes a difference, rather than merely spinning one's wheels. Again, the importance of dealing with the symbol world is that it's the understructure that connects. As such, growth in this area can have pervasive implications with a lasting impact.

Bear in mind, however, that the impact may not be immediate. The expansion of the representational world may take some time to settle in and find expression in a reality context. Since my efforts are not directed towards behavioral change and emphasize more of a growth orientation, concrete behaviors can be deceiving. I hope they can find a personalized sort of integration for their living, not a different behavior.

The term I use to describe how this really operates is "seeding the unconscious." I consider much of my input to the family to be akin to planting seeds in a field. If the seeds are hardy enough, the field fertile enough, and the conditions right, they may take root and grow. When the family and I click and make real contact, the seeds seem to do well, often bearing a harvestable fruit. When something is askew, they don't develop. But the actual harvest is theirs, not mine. They see it through and have the right to claim ownership of it. If I remain too invested in the outcome, it takes away from their capacity to really own the harvest.

The other component of seeding the unconscious that is so delicious is that I don't really need to do conscious battle with them to sow the seeds. I can slip in the ideas via a level of inference that doesn't arouse anything to concretely dispute or take issue with. Since I don't need to really convince them of my interpretation of them, I don't bait them into needing to counter my position. I don't find myself needing to play the therapist's trump card of labeling their disagreement with me as resistance. By not having a disagreement over who's really right, they're left with the experience. They've not been given the opportunity to disregard it based on an intellectual debate they feel they've won.

There are many ways to bring the benefit of confusion, or disorientation, into the sessions in a useful way. One of my favorites is to play with role confusion. I relabel the interactions I see in terms of roles, no matter who takes the parts. For example, to the young boy who is scolding Mom for not keeping her word I'll say, "Let's see. If you're your mother's father . . . the way you're correcting her you know . . . that makes you your own grandfather." Or to the wife who defers to her explosive husband, "You know, I bet he's so mad because you're not being a good enough mommy to him." This kind of playing with their roles, while sounding rather silly at first, often carries significant weight when they decide it's time to live differently.

Other ways include offering a string of ridiculous "solutions" when petitioned for an answer to a problem. This puts them in touch with their need to be responsible for themselves, instead of my acting as if I have the answer and am holding it until they can manipulate it out of me. Using double entendre words or unique phrases can also be powerful. Mixing literal and contextual meanings can also reveal covered underpinnings. For example, a new family came in with the husband blasting his wife for not buying him a fireplace starter for Christmas. He was livid that she had purchased one for her father and brother, but not for him. As she retorted by telling him how guilty he was making her feel, I commented, "You know, I just had a strange idea. As you were talking, I had an image of the fireplace starter as a sexual thing." They both burst into laughter and with an embarrassed look mentioned that the real reason they had come was that they were having sexual problems. Apparently the wife had been faking orgasms for years, only recently letting her husband know about it. Her husband truly could have used a firestarter.

I also strive to use affectively volatile words to attract attention and underscore issues. At times, overstating an issue is the only way to pull it out into the open. Accusing someone of being dishonest or, better yet, of being a liar may be needed to provoke a response. Asking where they acquired such a polished ability to deny problems with such a convincing smile can also draw a response.

Children often love my stories of what I did when I was a little girl. They can enjoy the silliness and often do a wonderful job of teaching their parents to loosen up. Only the most childish adults take themselves too seriously.

Experience

I've yet to meet the person who's been able to grow emotionally via intellectual education. True emotional growth occurs only as the result of experience. My next bumper sticker will read, "Nothing worth knowing can be taught." This isn't to say that learning and growth aren't possible, just that being presented with suggestions, recommendations or cognitive input is irrelevant. Not only that, it's frequently damaging to the process.

Insights and understanding happen as a result of experience, not as a precursor to it. As Kierkegaard said, "We live our lives forward but understand them only backwards." We must all reinvent the wheel if we're ever to benefit. It's much like that funny experience of becoming a parent. Until I had my first child, I knew all there was to know about raising children. Once I became a father, my knowledge crumbled and my learning began.

Growth

One of the ways I see families grow via this sort of work is in the emergence of an increased tolerance for the absurdity of life. They seem more able to transcend the pain they previously found unbearable. The fact that life remains painful no longer prevents them from living.

They're more able to face their fear, thereby breaking its stranglehold on them. It's like the idea that alcoholics drink because they're afraid of being afraid. Once you really face the terror that is real, you're free to live with it, not perpetually run from it.

Perhaps the best way to explain growth is to think of it as achieving a state of balance between belonging and individuating. Growth is a lifelong process of continuously striving for greater levels of belonging, as well as for increased individuation. The flux back and forth creates the flexibility to expand and add more of both. The more you dare to belong, the greater freedom you have to be independent. The greater your capacity to individuate, the more free you are to belong.

5

Getting Personal:
Challenging Rigidities
and Creating Pathways

Once you've completed the initial encounter and struggled with some of the beginning politics, the nature of the therapy process begins to shift. While the first date is often colored by the cure fantasy the family arrives with, by the next meeting the perspective changes. You're beginning to become a person, rather than a two-dimensional guru image. At this point I want to guide the evolving therapist-family suprasystem in the direction of more openness and honesty. I want it to become more personal.

My way of doing this is to respond to the family in a more personal way. When I'm able to become more personal in my responses to them, the sessions naturally move in that direction. There's a funny paradox embedded in the fabric here. When I find myself trying to be more personal or responding with the intent of forcing them to respond in kind, nothing happens. Contrived caring just doesn't work. It needs to emerge freely out of my growing capacity to experience their pain and relate to their struggle.

To even say that I'm trying to be more personal sounds too contrived. It's more a matter of my being more alive. If I can really be there, in the present, to get a personal sense of their pain, then I'm free to be instinctively responsive to what is occurring. My responsibility to the family is to be as personally responsive to them as I can. This is different from being responsible for or merely reactive to them. I'm not just acting in reaction to them, but I'm offering them a glimpse of my own internal responses as well. In other words, they're having the experience of my experience of me, not just feedback about them.

For example, at some point in the second interview the following kinds of comments often emerge:

Carl: Listen guys, I'm worried about us. I've sat here for the last 20 minutes without having any real sense of the pain you say you experience. We need to find a way out of this mess or I'll be of no use to you.

How can you draw me in enough to allow me to feel connected?

Carl: Wow! Is that ever frightening! The way you just looked at your husband. I was certain you really could run a knife through him if he ever hit you again.

What do you think, Jim? Is she finally over being a nobody?

Carl: You know, Jill, the way Larry gets so mad when you say you feel lonely makes me think he might really love you after all. Do you ever sense that too? That he just feels so inadequate that he takes it out on you?

Challenging the Family to Grow

As we reconvened the next morning, the family had regained its composure. Even so, the new day brought a tinge of tentativeness and uncertainty. How would we get started again? Who would take the lead? What are the expectations we all have? This is an important period! It's crucial that they take the responsibility for getting us under way. If I move in to cut the tension by providing a focus, it deprives them of the experience of taking charge of their own living.

After a few moments, Vanessa stepped in to get the ball rolling. She offered the topic of her parents trying to get too much parenting from their children. While it was slow to start, they were clearly making an effort. As they floundered about, the topic centered on Mom asking Marla for help in deciding what clothes to bring for the three-day experience. She then commented that she had forgotten her nightgown and her husband's nightclothes, too, for that matter. As she uttered those words, the visual image of Mom and Dad standing naked, rummaging through their suitcase, floated into my mind. I instinctively joined the discussion.

The nightgown talk and my association to it were enough to clue me in to the sexualized undertone of the moment. In a teasing manner, I more directly underscored the topic of sexuality. My intent was to make overt the covert undertones. This offers the opportunity to more clearly focus on an emotionally laden topic.

Van: You've been wanting some kind of assistance.

Dor: Caring.

Van: Marla said this morning that you wanted . . . you were putting clothes in a suitcase and you wanted to know what clothes to bring. You were asking Marla!

Mom: Yes.

Dad: Yes.

Mom: Yes. I didn't know what to take along. I forgot my nightgown anyway. I didn't bring his either.

Carl: You didn't bring his either? Boy, you guys have got troubles. What are you going to do tonight? You can get separate bedrooms.

(*laughter*)

At this point I am struck by the sexualized undertones. My comment is a response to this sense. I'm teasing them

about wanting to be naked
together and acting innocent.

Carl: The problems of old
folks get complicated.

Mom: They are! They really
are! It's just terrible!

Mom's comment verifies this
as an issue. Her capacity to
laugh at herself via the
exaggerated "It's just terrible"
gives consent for continuing
the overt focus on sexuality.

Van: I think it's kind of cute.

Carl: I think it's nice she could
admit it to you. Sex education
is a hard thing to come by.
Especially if you try to get it
from your mother.

Mom: That's one thing . . .
when I was pregnant with
Marla I tried to tell them
about babies. I don't know if I
told them enough.

Carl: He (Dad) probably just
told them it was like the cows.

Mom: I didn't really tell them
that.

Mar: Yes. Cows and bulls.

Mom: I told them more about
the delivery, not how it got
there.

Dor: You showed us some books.

Mom: Yes. I ordered some books but they were so deep that I couldn't even . . . I put them way up on the shelf. I don't know. But I did get books.

Carl: If you ever get very sex hungry, you can get a step ladder and get up on the shelf.

(*laughter*)

Dor: If you really, really need it!

Carl: You can't get it at the corner drugstore anymore.

(*silence*)

This loud, uncomfortable silence signaled their decreasing comfort with the topic of sexuality. At this point they must decide to press on or fall back.

With sexuality clearly the focus, Vanessa opted to take the risk of becoming more personal. This is a nice example of what I call "seeding the unconscious." By helping them face the sexual undercurrent, I've let them know that I realize it's a real issue. I'm willing to face it, but won't force it in a voyeuristic fashion. The choice is theirs.

Van: That's a hard area for me right now.

Carl: Sex education?

Van: Yes. Well, sex and love. They're separate. . . . I don't know. I have two images. One is to get married and have babies. That's painful and heavy and serious. You're tied into it and I don't want to have anything to do with it. The other part is that sex is fun and lively and it's fun to be single. It's like two totally different pictures.

When I start thinking about getting married, I have a lot of mixed feelings about it. I have a hard time finding a proper partner for myself. I really don't know if I choose the wrong person or if I repeat the same problem. I'm concerned about that.

Carl: Are you worried for fear you'll never make it?

(*laughter*)

The use of double entendre messages often results in a kind of double take. Such comments can lead to even more freedom and openness. In this situation, the whole family seemed to catch my play on the phrase "make it."

Van: Yes!

Carl: OK. Do you have any
sense that sex may prevent
loving?
I have this fantasy
that . . . one of the things I
struggle with with the younger
generation is . . . and I'm
like your mother's mother, I
feel antique . . . it's like a
penis and a vagina go off on a
trip together and there are no
people. I worry that the
people will never get there.

Again, the capacity to leave
them with another visual
metaphor, that of a penis and
a vagina on a date, is exciting.
Perhaps it will reveal something about the issue of sex
without love.

My comment about feeling
antique represents an effort to
avert being disqualified for
being out of touch. Since I've
declared myself stupid, their
need to do so is reduced.

Moving so quickly into a taboo topic like sexuality was somewhat of a surprise to me. It's rather unusual to have a conversation like this so early in therapy. It's an atypical pathway for
establishing a more open therapeutic relationship. Nonetheless, I had sensed it in their talk and opted to make it overt. It's
really a deciphering process, whereby I heard them talking
about sexuality via the metaphor of forgetting their night-
gowns. While they may not have been consciously aware of this
communication, it was clear enough to me.

This process of being open to my internal associations is central to my work. It's the way I can become personally involved. This also makes the session a real experience for me. I'm not crippled by the notion that I'm there just to help them. I'm also out to get something personal for myself. If I can remain free of the role of helper, the family can remain free of the need to be inferior. They can retain the courage required to explore their own lives with a sense of adventure. Vanessa displayed this capacity by so openly addressing her concerns about sexuality.

Her willingness to do this reflects not only her courage but also the fact that I took the risk of addressing sexuality. By sharing your own responses and reactions, new territories can be opened.

As the session continued, an interesting triangular dynamic among Vanessa and her parents surfaced. I want to help by tagging the pathological components of it. By breaking a rigidity, I hope to promote the development of a pathway.

Dad: Vanessa worries too much about things that don't affect her.

Carl: Like Mom's arthritis?

Dad: Yes, and like Gail and me not doing so well at home. I know she's sensitive. When I write a letter, she always follows up with a telephone call. Therefore, I don't write anymore. It riles her up and she gets concerned. The last letter I wrote, I forgot to put in the address and it came back.

Mom: I tell him, "Don't write her because she gets so worked up about the family." He tells her things aren't going so good. It makes it worse, you know. I just don't mention it.

Van: Well, I'd rather hear from you. I know I sometimes overreact.

Mom: You do overreact!

Van: I like to know what's going on.

Carl: You'd rather have the painful truth than Mom's nice lies?

Van: Yes!

Carl: Did you know about Mom's lying?

Van: Lying? No!

One of the ways families become stuck is to develop ways of avoiding real contact with each other. This is such an example. When information is withheld, upset may be avoided but distance is fostered. My effort is to explore this insidious process by tagging it with a less benevolent label. Calling Mom a liar forces it into the open and permits reevaluation.

Carl: She was just now saying,
"Don't tell her!"

Mom: I tell Dad not to tell
you.

Van: I've felt that you like to
keep secrets. I don't like it!
I know you want to protect
us, but I think it's hard on
you.

Mom: Yes. I'm the great
protector.

Carl: It keeps you making
believe they're still four or six.

Mom: What do you mean?

Carl: Well . . . that they're
too young to know!

Mom: Yes.

Van: You do. Sometimes you
treat us like we're real young.
Like we can't handle the
truth.

To really alter this process, it's
necessary to debunk the
notion that this serves a
positive function of protection. I'm helping them see it
as something that infantilizes
or inhibits growth. Once it is
so defined, the family will
move to correct it.

"Lying" is a special sort of word. It's a word that gets noticed.
It's a word that's difficult to ignore. When a word of such
intensity is selected, a discussion that might have passed and
been quickly forgotten is noted as being of significance. By
assaulting an interactive process that avoids intensity and

thereby diminishes intimacy, I'm clearing the way for a more open and honest pathway of communication.

I don't think you can get the same effect by being euphemistic. What needs to occur is an experience, something that is felt, not just comprehended. Besides, I'm not interested in being coopted into buying the family's style. They're skilled in averting crises by downplaying them. I need to challenge this appeasing style.

As the session continued, they began to settle into a comfortable topic of talking about Gail, the absent daughter. The session immediately deadened. I opted to challenge this status quo maintaining move. I wanted to block their effort to avoid the developing tension. When you remove the safety net of talking about an absent member, a void is created for them to fill. This means that those in attendance will need to step forward or have the session fall flat.

In this particular instance, I encouraged Vanessa to take a chance. Oftentimes I am less directive and wait for their decision.

Carl: Let me back you off a step. Let's talk about your craziness and not talk about Gail until she gets here. It's kind of unfair to talk about her behind her back.

(*pause*)

Van: OK. (*pause*) . . . One of the things I want to talk about is my relationships with men. I'm frustrated in trying to find a partner. Somehow I feel it relates to how I relate to Dad.

I just feel really, really sad and fed up. (*She begins crying and sobbing.*) I don't know how to meet anybody who really loves me. I can't stand it anymore!

Dad: Well, maybe that all stems from when you were born, because you stayed with Grandma.

Mom: Yes, maybe.

Van: I don't know.

Mom: It wasn't too good. We stayed with my mom for six weeks when I had her because I felt so weak.

As Vanessa moves into an area of great personal pain, her parents move to defuse the intensity. They move away from the present, opting for a historical topic. Vanessa persists, thereby creating a new path on the family map.

Van: I don't know if it stems from that. I just know it's hard to meet a man who loves me.

Carl: What about one you care about?

Van: I do meet them and then they just leave. They leave all the time, or they just reject me!

Mom: She comes on pretty

strong. She's aggressive. I don't know, a lot of girls are nowadays.

Dad: That's getting to be the trend.

Van: I just don't understand. I care a lot. I'm seeing this person Mark now. I care a lot, but he's not the right man for me. He's got another girlfriend.

Mom: Then you shouldn't monkey with him.

Van: I don't know why I keep getting involved with men who are unavailable. I've been doing this for 12 years. I'm really tired of it. When I turned 30, something clicked inside and I decided I've got to change this!

Dad: Yes.

Van: I gave myself a huge 30th birthday party. One of my friends, Peter, met one of my women friends and they went off together. I feel like I lost another man I was really starting to fall in love with. I feel it keeps happening!

Dad: Maybe you're like me in

that regard. I was older when
I finally got married.

Van: I was thinking about
that.

Mom: Yes. He had a lot of fun
until he was 33.

Dad: I retired when I got
married!

Carl: Good idea! It keeps you
from getting in trouble with
your wife.

Dad: The reason I got married
was because Mother had
passed away. I needed someone around the house. I knew
her family and that she was a
good girl. But I probably
wouldn't ever have married
if Mother wouldn't have
died.

Mom: He wouldn't have.

Dad: Some of the buddies I
chum with still aren't married.

Carl: You mean Vanessa won't
get married until you die?

This time Dad's comment is
more personal. It has a
quality of concern rather than
of evasiveness.

While Christ was crucified at
33, John was married.

This was an intuitive reply,
raising the possibility of an
affair as an issue to consider.
They chose to bypass it at this
time.

Dad: I don't know. She may marry late.

Mom: She will marry late!

This brief segment sheds some light on some of the family undercurrent. Vanessa may be struggling to avoid the kind of relationship she sees between her parents. She does so with such intensity that she, too, struggles.

Van: But it bothers me. I feel very frustrated.

Dad: That didn't bother me! If I was going with a girl and she went off and got married . . . Well, there's many pebbles on the beach. I made friends easily.

Van: I meet men easy too, but I don't choose the right one for a relationship. One was withholding and gave no affection. One went off with another girl. Now Mark has a girlfriend too.

Carl: Is he afraid you're going to eat him up?

This list of relationship failures seemed connected to the intensity of her need to find a partner.

My effort here is to provide a metaphor for how she might chase men off.

Van: I think a lot of men are afraid of my intensity.

Carl: Do you think you eat
them up to fill a hole inside of
you?

Van: Yes.

Carl: You can't fill a hole
inside you with someone else.

Van: I know! I have to do
something with myself. I
don't know how to fill it
though. I've been eating a lot
the past few days, trying to
fill myself up.

The whole business of family undercurrents and patterning
is quite powerful. The emotional relationship that exists between the parents often has profound implications for the children. Growing up in a family climate marked by distance and
noninvolvement between the husband and wife typically leads
to problems with intimacy for the children. In this particular
case, Dad's description of marriage as a matter of expediency is
striking. They struggle to avoid a similar fate, only to frequently find the same result.

Our capacity to struggle with these issues in a more overt
and direct fashion may create conditions that will permit
change. It may break the hypnotic-like spell that seems to hold
the children loyal to the family pattern. Facing the marital
distance and the attendant pain and isolation powerfully poses
the question, "Will I choose to follow this path?" It offers the
option of seeking a different type of relationship.

Later in the session, the broader network of family dynamics
was brought to the surface.

Carl: Did you know that if you
put your husband down it
would help your daughters

learn to put down their boyfriends?

Mom: Yes. It probably would. You mean in front of him? Sometimes I do behind his back.

Carl: Oh, I see. The truth comes out.

Mom: Well, he always walked away. He'd never sit and talk.

Carl: You could have tripped him as he walked out the door.

Mom: He says he's got to hurry outside. Then he'd usually get mad when I'd talk with Mike.

Carl: You mean Mike was your mother?

By labeling Mike as functioning in a mothering role with his mom, I hope to draw attention to the dysfunctional nature of the triangle. Again, this way of doing it is outside their normal style. It may have impact.

Mom: Yes. That's about it.

Carl: Boy! This is a confused family. Nobody knows who's who!

Mom: Mike and I could talk. He understands everything so clearly.

Carl: So if Mike is your
mother . . . (*laughter*) . . .
that means he's Marla's
grandmother.

Here I'm pushing the role
confusion. I want them to
really feel the absurd side of
some of their functioning.

Dor: Who's my brother?

Carl: It gets very complicated.

I'd like to talk more about this "technique" of playing with
the family roles. My intent is to expose some of the areas where
the roles or functions they serve are dysfunctional. Doing it in
this quasi-ridiculous manner often has the effect of allowing
families to clearly see the absurdity. The fact that Mike con-
soles his mother when she's distressed with her husband is a
problem. This sort of cross-generational alliance may be quite
damaging to the overall family. I want to disrupt their comfort
in maintaining this position, but don't want to "teach" them
how to be the ideal family. This sort of metaphoric tampering
with the family's destructive role structure leaves the real decision-making up to them. Their capacity to enter into some of
this absurdity is a sign that they can work with this sort of
prodding.

The idea that a therapist can "teach" a family how to function
better is patently narcissistic. I have enough trouble muddling
through my own life to feel I can bottle and export my own
brand of living. And to try to sell something that I'm not able to
live is psychopathic. The best I can do is to help them take a
look at themselves and to fully accept the responsibility for
deciding and living.

But it's not really turning them out in the cold. They have
inner resources and capacities to draw upon. It's my responsibility to trust that their resources exist and to nudge them to
look for them. Any other type of response is doing them a

disservice by assuming they are indeed barren and disconnected. The family emotional undercurrent is always there and invariably rich. It merely needs to be accessed. Even if there really are families without these assets, I've given up breast-feeding. It takes too much out of me!

Late in this session, Mom began discussing her frustration with Dad. She specifically addressed his behavior when they would attend dances. She complained that he would arrive with her but spend most of the evening dancing with other women. She stated that her husband would not listen to her protests and left her to be alone.

Carl: You didn't tell them that you were surprised that no one would dance with you unless they were drunk?

Mom: No, I didn't tell them that. It's true that it does bother me that no one will dance with me.

Dor: Why is that?

Mom: The arthritis, a little. They're afraid.

Dor: They're afraid to handle you?

Mom: But they see me out there dancing. But they don't want to . . . I am rigid. They're afraid, I think.

Dor: Well, one thing you could do is ask them to dance. If they're afraid to ask you . . . but if you come up to them and say, "I'm not going to break my leg!"

Carl: Or you could make Dad refuse to dance with anybody unless they get someone to dance with you.

Here I'm underscoring the fact that they are a couple. That the actions of one do have consequences on the other. I'm also prompting Mom to be less passive and to realize that she could act.

Mom: Yes. Well, that's what happens. I mean if a couple . . . he asks the woman to dance and the guy stands there or just walks away! It happens every single time. Doesn't it, Dad?

Dad: Yes, it does. Lately I haven't been dancing with too many others.

Carl: Why don't you tell the guy, "My wife's a good dancer and I like yours. Let's trade!"

(*quiet chuckling by the children*)

Mom: Yes.

Carl: "I'll see you for break-fast!"

(*laughter*)

I've now taken their social game and turned it sexual. By amplifying their scenario, I'm contaminating their comfortable lack of courage.

I want them to be more free to associate this dancing with a more profound infidelity. By letting them know that I believe their dancing has a sexual component, I've increased their anxiety. Their level of comfort has been contaminated. At the next dance, the game will be different.

Carl: We've got to stop.

Dad: Yes. That's a different approach.

(*laughter*)

Carl: You could offer to pay for the breakfast!

(*laughter*)

By having this exchange in the presence of the children, I'm destroying their fantasy of their parents as nonsexual beings. I want to free them to laugh at themselves.

By leaving the accusation of infidelity at the inferential level, they can't really reject it. Ending with things up in the air, with a sense of incompleteness or confusion, often leads to real integration and growth!

Again, this sort of seeding can have a powerful impact. The whole topic of infidelity has been broached in a way they could hear, but not feel pressured to reply to. If it turns out to be accurate, the reverberations will follow.

From a "technique" perspective, this sort of interaction can be considered an amplification move. I'm taking what they present, a repetitive problem at dances, and upping the ante by implying that it represents much more. This may have the effect of contaminating the comfort they have with the situation. It will change the context of the next dance. They're free to continue the game but not to not notice it!

*   *   *   *   *

Ques: Carl, this whole thing is wild! Are you really saying that dancing is a sexual affair?

Carl: Of course! I think . . . the idea that an affair has nothing but a penis and a vagina is crazy. We have psychological affairs all the time.

This man is having psychological affairs with all these people, dancing. Dancing is a sexual experience. You put your leg inside hers and she puts her leg inside yours. The thing I should have said but didn't is that maybe the men don't dance with her because she looks too sexy and they're afraid of getting an erection.

The whole idea of staying for breakfast, that's what I call seeding the unconscious. It's leaving them with an extrapolation from where their fantasy was, because my fantasy goes further.

Ques: Well, it really did seem like you were just pouring gasoline on the fire. That you were making it impossible for them to . . .

Carl: You can't have an orgasm if it doesn't get hot! You're just going to have to push these people. You can't just stay with their life. You're trying to augment their living to make it more successful and enjoyable.

Ques: Well, let me ask you a simple question. Why don't you just teach them? Why don't you just educate them and tell them straight out that they need to communicate better? That they need to be more respectful of each other? That they need to be nicer to each other?

Carl: Boy, am I glad you brought that up!

You know, that's the craziest idea, that education by a professional therapist is any different than education by the preacher, the Ten Commandments, the cultural mandate, the neighbor next door! You can't do that! Teaching . . . we are not able to handle our life by intellectual insight! It's got to be something more invasive. That's what the unconscious is all about. That's what this seeding their fantasy is all about. And you don't have to worry about too many seeds. That old business about Christ throwing the seeds . . . if they don't land right they won't grow. If they land right, they'll grow! Then whatever comes out will be harvestable. So I think it's very possible that this thing may hit them weeks later.

Ques: So you don't believe in education?

Carl: Maybe at the end of therapy you can begin to say things that because of your relationship are significant enough to last, but ordinarily education is not therapeutic.

6

The Universal Dilemma: Hopeless Men and Hopeful Women

Wife: Tell me you love me.
Hus: I love you.
Wife: You don't mean it!

Life is crazy! We scurry around in search of intimacy and personal involvement, only to shrink in terror when the possibility appears. It's often more comfortable to define ourselves by our social roles — I'm a therapist, or a father, or a husband — than to grapple with being human. The more we talk about being personal, the more firmly we cling to the role functions we've developed.

Just as each person must struggle with this dilemma, so too must each family. Every family consists of a complex matrix of values, images and myths concerning the territory of being human. How open are we with each other? How role-determined is our family? Can we face our impulses, or are they to be hidden? Are men and women more similar or different? Are children autonomous people or mere reflections of their parents? Is the extended family to be valued or feared? The issues are endless. The process of dealing with them eternal.

One of the affectively loaded issues in the family we're following is the whole topic of male-female relationships. How they relate, how distance is maintained, and how they seek intimacy are central issues. As we rejoin the sessions, Vanessa is talking about her previous involvement in an ashram and her struggles with men.

Van: I meditate every morning
for 10 minutes but I don't go
to any special practices or
groups or anything.

Carl: How did you get free? Or were you ever really captured?

Van: Oh, I was! I was really captured! I guess I turned from the ashram and meditation and those practices in order to put energy into my personal relationships.

Carl: How did you do it?

Van: My love relationships.

Carl: Oh boy! That's what I said in my discussion (*after the sessions yesterday*). That my suspicion was that your pain yesterday, with the boyfriend not succeeding, was that you were somehow trying to put the boyfriend in the place of the guru you used to have.

One of the real problems in life is to enter into relationships with the fantasy of being protected and taken care of. To expect a boyfriend to protect you from needing to be a real person is risky. If he fails, you're bitterly disappointed. Worse yet, if he succeeds, you're a nobody.

Van: I know. That's true. My boyfriend used to say that. He would say, "You get your boyfriends and your gurus confused."

Carl: Do you think you could make it without a guru?

Van: Or a boyfriend?

Carl: No, no.

Van: Just without a guru?

Carl: Yes. Because if you could make it without a guru, maybe you could have a boyfriend.

Mom: Right.

Van: I . . . I . . . I get scared about that. I feel like I want something to hang on to.

Here Vanessa is able to put words to the feeling of wanting to be protected. She wants to make believe she's a little girl again, this time getting the nurturance and protection she wants.

The intensity of her neediness suggests this is a good area to more fully explore. My effort is to tie these needs back to the family and her desire to get more from her father.

Carl: And you can't hold on to Dad?

Mom: Yes! That's exactly right!

Van: Yes. I don't know.

Carl: You said yesterday the boyfriend thing had something to do with Dad.

Van: Yes.

Carl: Do you think you can't hold on to him because he doesn't hold on to God as a guru?

Van: I don't know. I just don't feel really secure in my connection. I don't feel I can say, "Dad, I feel really scared!" I don't feel I have that kind of rapport with him.

Carl: When did you stop cuddling with Dad?

Van: Oh, I don't know! I don't know (*increasingly anxious*). I don't even know!

Carl: When you were little, huh?

Van: Yes.

Carl: Did you have any sense that he was afraid of having sexual feelings about you?

Van: Yes. I sensed that.

As we discussed her real difficulty in getting close to her father, she became highly anxious. This was especially pronounced when I asked about their cuddling together. My response was intended to bring this issue to the surface. By exposing the anxiety regarding the incest taboo, I hope to help free Vanessa to see her current life more clearly.

Carl: Do you have any idea when that was? Because it was very clear to me, it's become clear in later years, of course, that my mother got panicky about sexual feelings about me when I was 13.

By sharing this slice of my own life, I've normalized the issue of sexual feelings existing between parents and children. It tends to lessen their defensiveness.

This way of communicating is difficult to reject. They could have easily discounted any direct inquiries about incestuous feelings. When they hear me talking about my own life, however, they can't so easily invalidate it. It's part of me, not of them. But since it's also universal, it's about them too!

Van: mmmh hmmm.

Carl: Do you have any sense of what the age was when you and Daddy couldn't stand each other's excitement?

Van: I'd say sometime after 12. Twelve comes to mind.

The way Vanessa responded to my question regarding her lack of cuddling with Dad signaled this as a loaded area. Again, my natural inclination was to push it to a more anxiety-evoking level. To give the family the benefit of delving into new areas.

It's really not such a controversial issue, however. I'm merely making overt a universal reality. Bringing the impulses to light doesn't create them, it merely exposes them. Parents and kids do have sexualized feelings and impulses concerning each other. It's their panic to deny them that often makes them so dangerous. Cutting yourself off from your children in response to your own embarrassing impulses hurts the family. I want them to be able to face the impulse, not live in terror of it.

The decision to share with them this part of my own life is based on my belief that in order to really penetrate, you have to be personal. When I look at them, I need to be able to find part of me. When they look at me, I want them to find part of themselves. The capacity to see each other as human beings is central to any therapy. I don't concern myself with fears that they'll see me as inept or inadequate based on the information I choose to share. I'm not needing their approval or adoration in order to feel good about myself as a person. When you find yourself depending on feedback from your clients for your own sense of worth, you're in trouble. It precludes your being a therapist and leaves you in a sociopathic bind.

Actually, this whole business of trying to escape the professional dichotomy of "healthy therapist" and "sick patient" is an interesting phenomenon. Maintaining the dichotomy creates such a gap that real exchanges are minimized. It leaves clients with the belief that we can fix them and that they are defective enough to need fixing. Perhaps even more destructive is the delusion of grandeur it leaves imprinted on the therapist. It seems that the capacity of a therapist to be helpful is directly linked to accepting the fact that he can't help.

*   *   *   *   *

Ques: Carl, this was a heavy exchange. Here you were using your own life, your own experiences to talk about a very difficult and personal thing. Why did you delve into this whole question of incest? Even worse, why did you bring your mother into it?

Carl: Well, I think when you talk about the cross generational sexuality, you have to justify their exposing themselves by exposing yourself. If you don't, you're just being pornographic. You're just being dirty! If you expose yourself, . . . and I think you can only do that if you've had enough therapy so you're not asking for help with it . . . you're just reporting it as a past symbolic experience of yours. What it does is open the territory so they can think about it.

I try not to ask them to comment on their experience. I can ask her academic questions like, "How old were you when you think your father got scared," not saying anything about when she got scared. Then I can tell him about my experience with my mother, because it's a fact and it's discathected. I don't have any panic about it anymore.

Ques: But don't you run the risk of that making you sound like you're unhealthy? Like you've had this crazy relationship . . .

Carl: Of course I'm unhealthy! I have no intention of trying to fit into the myth of being healthy. I think of myself as being crazier than they are. Except I make an income at it and enjoy it! And I encourage them to be crazy. The problem is how to keep from being stupid!

Ques: Well, what's the difference? I mean, crazy and stupid . . . you make them sound different!

Carl: Well, if you're stupid and crazy, you end up in a state hospital. If you're smart and crazy, you end up like Picasso and make a contribution to the world. Or at least you earn a living like I do.

Ques: Well, it looks as if your approach worked here. It was powerful and maybe helpful. But there must be some guidelines around this whole issue. You don't just go around talking about your own relationship with your mother to any client you work with, to everyone you see. How do you know when to do it? How do you know when not to do it?

Carl: I don't decide ahead of time. I think one of the problems therapists frequently have is that they try to doublethink themselves. As soon as you doublethink . . . It's like asking the girl if you can kiss her. It's already too late. If you have to doublethink your therapeutic moves, then you're a fake. They'll then be a fake in response because they're going to doublethink their answers.

So this is how it comes. This is a creative experience for me. I assume it comes out of a clinical hunch.

Ques: It still leaves me uncomfortable! The idea that anything that pops into your mind during a session comes out of your mouth?

Carl: Sure. Sure. Let me see if I can tell you . . . there ought to be some training involved in that. This 20, 30, 40 years of background that I come from makes me much more comfortable and confident of my interventions. The first 10, 15, 20 years I was protected, guided, trained by a cotherapist to modify, to disagree, to agree, to give me the kind of freedom I needed because the therapist was the twosome.

Just like the single parent thing, the single therapist is sick. The family is too powerful for one therapist. There needs to be a pair of parents. And there needs to be a pair of therapists. As you get older, as you get to be a grandmother, you can raise a child by yourself. As I get to be a grandfather, I can treat some families by myself. But I would much rather have a partner and let the team do the work.

*   *   *   *   *

As the session continued, the focus on Dad's capacity for per-

sonal involvement emerged. We learn that he felt squeezed out
by his Dad in parenting his own children.

Carl: How about that, Dad?
Do you remember the times
when you used to be able to
cuddle with your oldest
daughter?

Dad: Well, Grandpa more or
less took over. He did that all
the time.

Carl: We old men are very
seductive. We get so hungry.

Dad: He wanted somebody
close.

Mom: He wanted someone to
hold on to and he did. He
cuddled all of them. Dad
didn't cuddle any of them.

Dad: No.

Mom: I used to hand Dad the
kids and he'd just hold them.
He'd just hold them and not
cuddle them. He just held
them.

Carl: Men are very discouraging.

Mom: Yes.

Carl: That's why they talk
about a second childhood.
Because most men give up

being human beings during
their working lives. When
they get old they realize what
they missed and start franti-
cally trying to get closer to
someone. Have you had any
sense of that with him?

Mom: A little bit, maybe.

I'm offering Dad the opportunity to look at the current
status of his life and dare to
look at his loneliness.

    Men often seem to try to
survive by remaining numb
to real life and acting like
they're things rather than
people. I'm offering Dad a
glimpse of his humanness as
an alternative to remaining
numb.

Carl: Of course, it's complicated with you because he can
cuddle with your mother
because she's nonsexual. She's
like his mom.

Mom: Right. He was very
attached to his mother. He
and his mother were like this
(*Mom crossed two fingers*), and
his dad was out.

Carl: I had the craziest
thought. (*laughing*) When you
said he and his mother were
like this (*crossed fingers*), I was
seeing the gnarled fingers and
that there was something

gnarled between him and his
mother.

By sharing my imagery, they will be left with a clear picture of something unhealthy between Dad and his mother.

   This reflexive sharing of another of my visual images is in-dicative of my growing capacity to be free with them. We've gotten beyond the initial political phase. While politics always remain a part of the relationship, they now recede into the background.

   It's like any other relationship in terms of growing by stages. Now I'm less tied up in their reality struggle and more free to be in touch with my own internal reactions. This is an essential phase to reach if our sessions are to be fruitful. To the extent that I'm captured by their reality dilemma and solution search, I'm coopted into their system. Once inside, I'm neutralized. Once seduced in this way, my efforts resemble those of Alice, who while running with the Queen of Hearts exclaimed, "The faster I run, the further behind I get!"

Men/Women: The Eternal Dialectic

The old axiom, "Men use love to get sex, while women use sex to get love," seems to have some merit. It exemplifies the basic, primitive, differing perspectives held by the male and female elements of many cultures. While in today's modern, sophisti-cated society this may be perceived as being old-fashioned, the human evidence is hard to refute.

   Men just have an impossible time with intimacy. Rather than seeking meaning through personal relationships, men pursue it by achievement, acquisition, and possession. Much like the little boy who collects model cars or baseball cards, big boys do the same thing. The toys change to money, or sports cars, or companies . . . it's all the same. Men dress themselves in accomplishments and successes. Without them, they feel naked and ashamed. They define themselves by what they have, not by who they are. The very question of who they are even sounds ludicrous. What does it really mean?

But there's more! Men seem to need this type of focus to protect them from something that's terrifying. The very idea of really letting someone know you is too threatening to even acknowledge. When men are with other men, that's not so tough. They really focus on matters that are of some importance. You know, how the Dodgers did, what's up with the Packers, what's happening on the stock market, take a look at my new car, did you see the new secretary at work?

This level of relating, or non-relating if you prefer, seems perfectly acceptable for most men. It begins to break down only when you bring women into it. Women seem to know that intimacy is possible and worthy of pursuit. I suppose it goes back to the private relationship women have with their children in utero. As that relationship develops, it becomes a profound experience for the mother. The father is usually unaware until the baby is born. I'm not sure they ever really catch up. Certainly, the historical division of labor, where the man went out to slay the dinosaur while the woman protected the children in the cave, contributed to this imbalance.

Despite the objections of our current culture, I believe that biology transcends psychology. Men can certainly learn to be more personal and nurturing, but I doubt that they can ever really become as intuitively caring as a mother. Even tampering with the traditional sociocultural model won't really do the trick. I use the analogy of a bicycle wheel to describe the traditional family model. The mother is the hub of the wheel. She is responsible for the inner world of the family, for seeing to it that there is sufficient nurture and caring. The father is the actual rim and tire. His function is to deal more directly with the outside world. He is to protect the rest of the family from some of the dangerous aspects of the real world, as well as to prepare the kids to be able to negotiate the demands of that world. The kids then are the spokes. They're what join Mom and

Dad together. I suppose they also tend to keep them apart if we press the analogy too far. In any event, this model is not one that fosters intimacy between Mom and Dad as husband and wife.

In rejoining the family, their idiographic version of this universal issue comes to light.

Carl: The real problem is, with most men, that they give up hope of really getting anything out of life when they're very young. They're trained to fall in love with things. With machines and animals and work.

For the male, who from early on is taught that emotional involvement is frivolous, life becomes a challenge to find safe areas, issues or objects to invest in.

Mom: Yes! Yes! That's exactly it! He's in love with his tractor. When it was out of kilter and didn't work, he moaned, "Oh! I've got to have that tractor. You know I need that tractor!" So Mike had to fix it.

Carl: With a passion.

Mom: Yes! With a passion! That's his passion!

Carl: Do you have any sense of when it was that you gave up on trying to humanize

him? How long after marriage
before you decided he was
hopeless?

Mom: Oh, not right away.

(*laughter*)

This comment underscores
the typical struggle of early
married life. The woman tries
to help the man live in the
present. To become involved
with her on a personal level.
Their laughter confirmed
their recognition of the
struggle and, perhaps, the
despair of its reality.

Carl: Well, it usually isn't
right away because usually
the woman confuses sex with
love. She doesn't realize the
man isn't really loving, he's
just sexual.

Mom: Right. Well, it must
have been at least a couple of
years. Maybe five years.

My effort here is to bring Mom back into the equation. Now
that we've established men as being hopeless, I want Mom to be
free to look at the reality of her living. To really face the fact
that her husband doesn't share much tenderness with her. That
she's alone.

Being fooled by a man's interest in sex is one of the oldest
ways women try to convince themselves that they're cared
about. While it's temporarily reassuring, it's dehumanizing in
the long run.

I work from the assumption that before Mom can really
mobilize herself to grow, she will need to face the reality she
tries to ignore. Only then can her pain and loneliness become

allies in her struggle to grow. Only then can they give her courage and direction. Until she can embrace the pain, it will keep her frozen and isolated. Of course, embracing it will also be painful, but it's a pain with some promise and hope, not debilitating in nature.

Carl: . . . and ever since then you've been depressed?

Mom: I don't know. I know since I've had rheumatoid arthritis I've been depressed. For 14 years now.

Carl: Is it getting worse?

Mom: I don't know.

Carl: Let me ask you a crazy question that just popped into my head. Do you think Gail's sickness has kept your arthritis from getting worse?

Mom: Maybe a little bit. I don't know.

Carl: That's how I think about families.

Mom: I don't have time to think of myself because of her.

Van: You also yell at Gail a lot. You get a lot of anger out at her.

Mom: Yes. I do pick on her.

Carl: So you're really having

an affair with Gail, while he's
having an affair with the
tractor?

Mom: Maybe.

Again, psychological affairs
are marked by an intense
investment of affect. This one
may have the benefit of
allowing Mom to express
some of her pent-up rage, but
it is self-defeating in the long
run.

This is a clear example of the double levels of impact that fill
our lives and create the paradoxes we struggle with. While on
the surface it appears that Mom's capacity to dump on Gail
may at least relieve her anger, at deeper levels it turns back on
her. Nothing is really resolved and a triangulated interactive
system is reinforced.

Given this way of interacting, Gail is now employed. While
the pay is low, there's a lot of status in being your mother's
primary object of intensity. The automatic consequence of never being able to grow up is a small price to pay for the lifetime
security of being so desperately needed. Part of the problem is
that while Mom may indeed get some relief, at a deeper level
she knows she's hiding from the real issues that trouble her. She
may even have some awareness of actively perpetuating them.

Beyond this, it's not even healthy for Dad to get off the hook
so easily. He needs to feel that he's wanted . . . whether it be
dead or alive. Being wanted is an essential part of life. Their
distance certainly maintains his comfort level, but also greatly
contributes to his sense of meaninglessness.

Perhaps the most devastating component of this sort of family style relates to their unwillingness to really face themselves
and the relationship issues that will be passed on to future
generations. The fantasy that you can escape unscathed is absolutely disastrous!

Carl: Where else is there passion in the family? I had a feeling when Dad made a crack about . . . Is it Marla? Is that your name? . . . Crazy! My grandmother was named Marla. That's why I wasn't sure. When Dad made that crack about Marla's drinking yesterday, I had the feeling there was a real passion fight between them.

Is that true? That Dad's worried about your future? He thinks you're going to end up being a bad girl and he's trying to beat you into submission, so you'll be a good housewife for some farmer?

Mom: I think that's right.

Mar: I never thought about it before. I suppose it could be.

Mom: Yes, he's worried.

Carl: Can you fight him? Can you stand up to the old man?

Mar: Yes.

Carl: Can you really ever win?

Mar: Not really.

It was my impression that Dad's complaint about Marla's drinking was a way of saying he was invested in what happened to her. While

it was controlling in form, it
showed some type of caring.
Perhaps the only kind he's
been able to permit himself to
share.

Carl: Not really, huh? When
he wins and you look
bad . . . does he ever come
back and apologize when he
discovers he was wrong?

Mar: No.

Carl: Have you ever asked
him to?

Mar: No.

Carl: What do you think
would happen if you did? If
you came back to him 24
hours later and said, "Look! I
looked that thing up in the
encyclopedia, you old so and
so, and you were wrong! Just
plain wrong! You shoved it
down my throat until I had to
give up. Now I want you to
apologize." Did you ever do it?

Mar: No.

Carl: What do you think
would happen?

Mom: None of us have.

Mar: Probably nothing.

Here I want to plant the idea
that there are ways to ap-

proach the old man. He's not dead yet.

Carl: Well, I wouldn't be surprised, he might be getting old enough that if you really put it to him straight, he might have more guts than you give him credit for.

Or more love, if I can use a clumsy term.

Do you think he loves you?

Mar: Yes.

Carl: In his own way, huh?

Now I want to help them acknowledge the loving, caring side of the family. While it's not easy to see, I know it's there! If I can help them look at it, they'll be more able to treat each other like people, not role functions.

Carl: Do you think he loves Mom?

Mar: Yes.

Having gotten one admission, I push ahead to the big game. I want to force them to directly face the question, "Does Dad really love Mom?" It's something they all shy away from and leave unsettled. They need to deal with it!

Carl: Because I didn't believe that crap yesterday about it being a marriage of convenience! I think it's a way they fool themselves about their investment in each other.

It may not be the kind of love they'd like, but I don't think you can keep from investing in each other. And I don't think you can withdraw your investment! Even when you get divorced and remarry two or three new people, one after the other.

Marriage is a process that intertwines people in a profound way. The shared living that ensues is real, with deep roots. Despite the popularity of divorce, I don't believe you really ever eradicate the root system.

You can fall in love but I don't think you can ever really fall out. This boyfriend you're breaking up with will always be in your head. You can decide not to live your life with him, but that's different. You still have him in your guts.

Mom: I'm sure it bothers her!

(*Marla is tearful.*)

Carl: The nice part about loving is that it's not like soap. You don't use it up. It's more like muscles, the more you learn to love, the more you can love.

It's the craziest thing the way our culture views marriage. It's as though we believe it's possible to live a shared life together without becoming emotionally involved or invested. It's simply not possible! Living together for years automatically involves a rubbing off and sinking into each other. While it may not be ideal, it is real.

I believe we select partners we are psychologically matched with. It's not really a random process at all. I don't believe we end up married to a particular person by mistake. The excuse of "temporary insanity" doesn't fit with my experience. Of course, there typically is massive collusion in this process, whereby we mutually agree to be a certain way with each other as part of the sales effort. His temper somehow doesn't show until after the ceremony. Her perfectionism is viewed as neatness until it's turned on him during the honeymoon. But to say that they were completely unaware, to infer that they truly didn't realize what they were getting into, is ridiculous.

While on the surface it appears that we select someone who will meet all of our needs and make us whole, the real relationship lies deeper. Paradoxically, the more clearly our selection seems to meet our surface needs, the more profound will be the struggle to really become a healthy couple. It often seems that by virtue of our marriage selection, we are faced with the opportunity to struggle with some of our most terrifying fears. Marrying a spouse because his strength makes you feel secure eventually comes around to your needing to challenge and defeat his strength in order to be a person. As you defeat his strength, he must then face the fears and uncertainties it masked. Selecting a wife because she's so thoughtful and attentive to your needs ends up in the dilemma of being bored by her lack of individuality. The twists are endless, with tremendous variations and diversity of style.

Despite the struggles that follow, it may be that these difficulties are central to developing a real sense of intimacy. After all, intimacy is a process, not an event. It's something that develops and evolves over time, it doesn't just exist. When marriage can provide the security needed to bilaterally face your own inner fears, as well as those of your spouse, intimacy follows. Getting mired down in a bilateral projection-of-blame process does little to encourage growth.

As we rejoin the family, all the women are crying over the pain of Marla's struggle with her boyfriend. As usual, Dad appears untouched.

Carl: That was a very nice thing. It was very nice for me yesterday, the way you guys can cry.

I think it's too bad you haven't been able to teach the old man how.

Mom: He won't cry.

Carl: Maybe you can get him to cry about the tractor someday.

My comment here exposes a raw nerve in the family. While the women got involved, Dad ducked out.

Mom: Oh, he will! I know he will!

Dad: Yes! When I can't drive it anymore!

Carl: When you can't drive it anymore? Well, I . . . it's funny, my thought was, when I was about 10, . . . I started driving the tractor when I was about 7. When I was 10 I missed a curve. We had an old Case (tractor) and it didn't turn very well. I went

over a bank into the river,
about up to my belly. The
entire tractor was underwater.

Here, in reaction to Dad's
surge of affect regarding the
tractor, I followed his lead.
While it was an automatic
reaction, my personal vignette
served to amplify the oppres-
sion they typically feel regarding Dad's tractor talk.

Van: I don't want to talk about
tractors anymore!
(*angrily screaming!*)
I don't want to talk about
goddamned tractors! I want
to hear about how Marla's
doing! I don't want to hear
about tractors!

  Jesus Christ! Somebody's
in pain here! I don't want to
hear about tractors!

  I want to hear about
Marla. I want to hear about
her boyfriend!

Dad: Yes. That's true enough.
But sooner or later you have
to have material things too.

Van: Well, I want to hear
about Marla. I don't want to
hear the two of you talk about
fucking tractors! I don't give a
fuck about them!

Vanessa's explosion in opposi-
tion to this now exaggerated
family style is intense. It's her
way of fighting Mom's battle

and of sharing more of her
desperation about men.

My joining Dad led her to
panic that all men are hopeless. That all men basically
view her as a tractor. If she
works well enough, for sex or
whatever, they're interested.
If not, they're occupied
elsewhere. Dad's response to
her passionate plea was
discouraging.

*   *   *   *   *

Ques: Carl, when Vanessa had that blowup, why didn't you
move to console her? It looked like you just ignored her
pain!

Carl: Of course! Had I consoled her, I would have been the
mother, not the father. I would have represented the caring person she wanted, rather than the uncaring person
she needs to learn how to get through to. She's trying to
find a man who's a human being. Finding me wouldn't
help. She needs to find her father! She needs to dare to be
personal with him.

This had a strange kind of personal quality. She's rag-
ing at him, but that's at least explosive in character, not
hopeless and dissociated like he is.

Ques: You know, that whole idea of men being hopeless seems
like an antiquated concept. Haven't we, in the last few
generations, come a long way from there?

Carl: I don't think we've come an inch! I think that old classic
cliché . . . that the only difference between men and
boys is that men's toys cost more. Whether it's an air-

plane, or satellite, or psychiatric theory. I don't think it makes a bit of difference. I think we're still in the play-pen, where our mother left us.

*   *   *   *   *

A pronounced, painful silence followed Vanessa's outburst. Only Marla's muffled sobbing interrupted the silence. Mother spoke first, in an instinctively protective maneuver to relieve the tension.

Mom: Part of it is that at every meal . . .

Carl: Let her talk, Mom.

I want to afford them the luxury of being able to more fully experience the pain. Perhaps they will be able to get some benefit from it if they don't flee so quickly.

(*silence*)

Mar: I don't know if I should break it off with him.

Mom: Did you tell him?

Mar: Not yet.

Carl: Do you want to break up because the family says so, or because you want to?

Mar: Because I do. The family probably doesn't want me to.

Carl: Is it clear to you that you can break up with him

and go back to him in five
years if you want to?

Mar: I don't know.

Van: Do you feel that you
don't like him anymore?

Mar: No, I don't feel that.

Mom: Then why do you want
to break up with him?

Mar: I don't know. I don't   Marla reveals a painful
want to get that involved with   reality of the family. The
anyone! (*Dad passes the box of*   reluctance to get involved
tissues.)   because of the pain it might
                                      bring.

Mom: He's pretty serious
about you. It will be hard for
both of you.

Dad: Yes. It will be hard. I
like the fellow.

Later in the session, I'm talking with Vanessa about her
problems with men. She talks of her typical style of approaching until she feels the man might really be there for her. At that
point she retreats.

Carl: Are you afraid that
if you don't retreat, you'll
get stuck like your mother
did?

Van: Yes. That's definitely   Here I'm drawing attention to
true!   the cross-generational influ-
                                      ences. This may serve to fuel
                                      a real effort to change.

Carl: So why don't you help

your mother learn to stand up
on her hind legs and fight
Dad?

Van: I've been trying to, in
different ways over the years.
I guess that's why I wanted
these family sessions. I don't
know how to stand up to Dad
myself!

Mom: Nobody does! Nobody
knows how to! No one in the
neighborhood will fight him.
What he says goes!

Carl: Marla said she does. She
just can't win, but she stands
up.

Mom: No one can win.

Carl: Well, you horrible old
bastard, what are you going
to do about yourself?

Dad: Live as long as I can,
then . . .

Carl: Then you're going to
die, huh?

Dad: Well, I suppose there's
no alternative. It's inevitable.

Here I've put their rage at
Dad in more graphic words,
hoping to push the process.

Carl: Do you suppose she'll
get over her arthritis when
you die?

Dad: Could be.

Mom: I don't think so.

Carl: Do you think she has a younger man on tap? Maybe she's sort of waiting for you to get out of the way so she can have a happy life.

Dad: I wouldn't know that. But there are boys around.

Carl: Have you suspected that?

Dad: Well, I more or less encourage people to not depend entirely on one person. Sooner or later you're going to need someone to carry on. Like in her condition, it would be very bad for her and the rest of the family if she didn't have somebody to hold on to.

Carl: Maybe she could go into a bar and ask for someone.

As Dad continues to define the issue as a nonissue, I continue to probe. While no impact is apparent, it may take later.

Van: I think she depends on Mike.

Mom: Yes. Right.

Dad: Sure.

Van: It makes it hard for Mike to get relationships going.

Carl: That's why he didn't

come? He didn't want to
expose that he's Mom's new
man?

Van: He'll be here tomorrow.

Carl: Yes, but . . . you know.

Mom: I know. He doesn't want
to come.

With the broader family now
in focus, the heat increases.
Mom reveals her way of
coping with Dad's distance.
She shares the centrality of
her son in her life. Dad again
opts for irrelevance by turning
to reality.

Dad: That's bad. If you
depend too much on . . .

Mom: He's the only one who
understands me! He under-
stands the whole situation.
He sees it all as clear as a bell.
As clear as a picture!

Dad: When I pass on, someone has to take over. Of
course, he's taken over the
farm already.

Mom: It's too much for him!

As the session begins to wind down, Vanessa and her mother
revisit the impossibility of dealing with Dad. While the theme
is an old one, their increased willingness to discuss it in front of
him is encouraging.

Mom: I don't like it. I can't get
to him. He walks away. If he

stays, he turns on the radio
with Paul Harvey real loud.
He just eats and eats . . . or
he'll leave. I just can't talk to
him about human things.

Van: I guess that's why I really
reacted about the tractor talk.
(*looking at Dad*) I got angry
when you wouldn't talk or
wouldn't listen to what
Marla's going through, or
what Mom's going through.
You want to talk about farm
things and we have to listen to
your conversation.

We're eating dinner, and
you're talking about the
weather. There are more
important things to talk
about. I know it's hard to talk
about things. I know we
didn't get much out of Marla,
but I feel we need to try.

Mom: I've always said, I'm
sick and tired of being at the
table with the two men. All
they talk about is work and
the weather. The tractor and
bolts. I always interrupt 100
times a day.

Carl: You really haven't given
up yet, huh?

Mom: No.

Carl: But just using a rubber
hammer against a stone wall?

7
The Secret to Unhappiness: Getting What You Want

"The only thing worse than not getting what you
want is getting what you want."

The truth found in this seemingly ridiculous statement is indeed terrifying. We all work and struggle to achieve certain goals. We sacrifice to get there, only to discover that the joy we expected is fleeting and elusive.

Although repetitively chronicled throughout history, why should it be so for me? Aren't I different? Won't I find real joy in reaching my goals? Perhaps the bind lies not in the idea that achievement is useless, but in the notion that through it life will be made easy. That I will live without heartache, pain, or sorrow. This belief is destructive! A more productive perspective would be to strive to transcend the pain by accepting it. Only by embracing pain are we free of its grip. As Sheldon Kopp so succinctly put it, "You can run but you can't hide."

The reason getting what you want is so devastating is that the want is so misguided. When we focus on accomplishment, we're doomed to fail, even in success. When we pursue illusory goals, the response will come in kind. Only by your facing your struggles and accepting your responsibility can real growth begin.

As the sessions resumed, the family was discussing a similarity between the generations regarding a dating pattern. As Doris and Vanessa spoke of both dating the same guy, sequentially of course, Mom mentioned that Dad had dated her sister before marrying her.

We soon were enjoying the coming to light of this previously hidden pattern. I suggested that perhaps Marla and Gail deserved a chance at the ex-boyfriend too. As we talked, a visual image formed in my mind. As is my usual style, I shared it

147

with them. Since it was our mutual exchange that triggered this image, I considered us full partners. It belonged to them as much as to me.

Carl: Gad zukes! Me and my crazy ideas. My next picture was one of those motel bedrooms. It has two double beds in the same room.

(*pause*)

It seems too crazy for even me. I never have been quite clear what the message is with all these motels having two double beds in one bedroom.

Mom: Yes. I don't know.

Carl: It sounds like musical beds.

Mom: I . . . when we went to my brother's wedding, it was my Mom and I and there were two double beds. I thought it was weird. Why couldn't they have single beds?

Carl: Yes. Or at least supply boyfriends.

Mom: Yes. That's what it is.

Carl: You should have checked with the manager.

Mom: Yes. I didn't check. I

don't like that idea anyway.
Sour grapes, I suppose.

This kind of teasing can serve a vital function. It establishes a set whereby communication can occur more openly, with less conscious screening.

Mom's willingness to engage in this sort of give and take reflects a developing trust. She's more willing to risk.

Given this emerging atmosphere of openness and risk taking, Vanessa decides to take another chance. She further pursues her boyfriend struggle. She asks for help.

Van: So, Carl, I don't know where I am with my boyfriend problem. I don't know what to do!

Carl: Did you expect to have a solution?

Van: Well, yes. I kind of want some kind of solution.

Carl: Oh? Merry Christmas!

(*laughter*)

Here Vanessa's fantasy of being taken care of, or of getting a solution for her living, surfaces. While it's a seductive offer to be her guru, or husband, or whatever, it's also treacherous!

My response of "Merry Christmas" is a short-hand way of saying that she'll have to be her own Santa Claus.

This is a Battle for Initiative exchange. My goal is to force her to take responsibility for her own living. To let her know that she will need to take full responsibility for her own style of living.

Carl: That's a great fantasy! I tell you what . . . I just thought of a solution. Become a lesbian!

Van: I've thought of that.

Carl: You see? Why are you asking me? You already have the answer. Then you won't have to worry about boyfriends at all!

Van: But that didn't work.

Carl: That didn't work? Well maybe it's because you didn't find the right woman.

Van: I thought of that.

Carl: Do you know . . . I never thought of that . . . do you think that incest between sisters would be taboo?

(*laughter*)

Between brothers it is, but I don't see how it could be between sisters.

My tongue-in-cheek offering of a variety of nontraditional "solutions" is meant to further convince her of the need to make her own decisions. I don't want to treat her as if she's stupid.

Carl: Life is getting so complicated! We could go back to the good old days when everybody knew what was right and wrong. What the rules were.

Mom: They broke them then, too.

Carl: Well, that was something else. As long as you knew them, it didn't matter if you kept them or not. It's like the Ten Commandments are a final exam. Answer any five.
      What did you say, Dad?

Dad: Well, in the old rules and even now . . . you take the Amish for example. They're so very strict, but still they have prematerial sex!

What a beautifully male slip this is! Talking of prematerial rather than premarital sex is vividly revealing.

Carl: Really?

Dad: I just found that out not too long ago.

(*laughter*)

Carl: Is that why you're

wearing those overalls? So
you can be Amish?

Dad: No, but I went to an
auction not long ago . . .

Carl: And one of the Amish
women propositioned you?

Dad: No, but some people
seen some Amish there. They
were talking there and I was
listening in. That's what they
were saying. I don't know!

Carl: You don't know, huh?
You should go to another
auction and find out!

Dad: They go out and check
the women before they get
married.

Mom: To see if they can
reproduce, I suppose.

Dad: Even the Quakers! You
should check the Quakers.

Carl: Even the Quakers, huh?
Maybe I should check them.

Dad: I don't know, but I read
something about them.

Carl: My wife is very jealous.

Dad's entry at this point
reveals his interest in his
daughter's struggle. His
comments endorse the validity
of her search.

The absurd, ridiculous,
almost whimsical quality of
this discussion is encouraging.

> The family has momentarily transcended the heaviness of living and are free to play in a world of possibilities.

*　　*　　*　　*　　*

Ques: Merry Christmas? Come on, Carl, what do you mean Merry Christmas?

Carl: Well, it's a way of saying something that indicates the absurdity of the question. It's responding to her in a way that she can't do anything with.

　　Life is difficult and the sense of the absurd is a way of seeing over the top of it.

Ques: But she was asking you, "Is there going to be a solution to this? Can you help me with a solution?"

Carl: And if I said no, that would be no help. If I said yes, I'd be lying. What I was saying is, unask the question. Don't talk like that! You're not a little five-year-old. You're an adult. You know there's no solution. I'm not going to tolerate your toying with me. I'm going to toy right back!

Ques: But why did you move to all the crazy alternatives? To all the ridiculous possibilities that you listed?

Carl: Because she opened up the sense of futility that is crazy. She opened up her ambivalence, her indecisiveness, and I offered the crazy alternatives that would get her past her fear of her own craziness.

　　We all have our inner life and our outer life. We're afraid to join the two. So I was producing an inner life fantasy of mine that she didn't have to agree with or even join with. But she could see that it was alright for me to think like that and thus she could be a little freer to think like that herself.

Ques: So you make this whole thing sound like parallel tracks of some kind. That you move along the same course, the same path that they do.

Carl: That's right! The response to an absurd question should be an absurd answer.

*   *   *   *   *

I'd like to say more about this whole business. This sphere of absurdity and ridiculousness must not be confused with irrelevance or tangential wanderings. It's really a way of going deeper. Of going beyond the limitations of the reality dimension and triggering a more pervasive and profound type of response.

In this particular example, Vanessa was asking for a concrete solution to her boyfriend dilemma. This is an issue she's struggled with for years without satisfaction. I sensed an undercurrent expectation or wish on her part that the answer could be provided by someone else. She's engaged in a desperate search to find the guru who could offer the wisdom she seeks, but she's failed to really look within herself. No doubt others have attempted to meet her request and provide the direction sought, but to no avail. I'm not interested in adding my name to the list of well-intended but misguided advice givers. I want to be useful, not insulting to her! To respond at the surface level would really be a way of saying that I agree that she's too stupid to find her own solution.

I've often thought that as far as therapists go, the worst vice is advice. It's a way of stroking our own ego by acting as if we really do know a better way, and reinforcing the one-down position of the client. While a seductive proposition, it has little to do with the goal of growth. In fact it actively impedes it!

So I want to pop this fantasy balloon. To force her back into herself as her own guru. In a sense, to begin to take herself more seriously and develop some self-respect. My "Merry Christmas" reply is a concise way of bringing to the surface her fantasy expectation of being given the gift of a solution. She must accept the job of being her own Santa Claus! It's much like Dorothy in *The Wizard of Oz*. She placed all of her hopes in the fantasy that the Wonderful Wizard would save her. As it turned out, she had the solution all the time, without realizing it. For that matter, so did the Lion, Straw Man and Tin Man. I want to help her realize it!

Perhaps the Wizard had a similar view. After all, when first petitioned to fulfill their wishes, he sent them out to get the broomstick of the Wicked Witch of the West before permitting an audience. In other words, he pushed them to go through a process that would require that they use the very resources they thought they lacked. I'm up to the same business. I want to push them back into their own resources. One way of doing this is to not only decline their invitation to point the way, but to actively offer a number of "solutions" that will force a reliance on their own latent resources. This highlights the ridiculous nature of asking someone else to solve your dilemmas. The more absurd my suggestions, the more they will accept the need to guide their own ship.

But it's more than merely being ridiculous or cynical or uncaring. The very process of my refusing to take over is in itself an act of caring . . . but a different kind of caring. In this one maneuver, I'm telling her that I won't even try to tell her what to do and that I believe that she has all the resources needed to complete the journey. It's this kind of confidence that offers the support needed to press forward. It's similar to the kind of parenting children need as they are faced with the need to make her own decisions about life. They don't need you to decide for them, so much as for you to help them with the process of deciding. To supply them with the undercurrent sense of support they need.

This type of struggle produces a type of second order change that no amount of professional advice could ever approach. It leaves the client with the realization and acceptance as well as the confidence needed to make her own decisions and live with the consequences. By avoiding the reality trap, Vanessa is more free to take herself seriously in creating a new reality. To tie this to a term we've earlier discussed, it's a Battle for Initiative issue.

As the session continues, Vanessa shifts from searching for a solution to the boyfriend dilemma to saying that she no longer wants to be a parent to her parents.

Van: (*to her parents*)
Being back with the family
for this visit gets me feeling
that I need to take care of you
again.

Dor: I sometimes feel that,
too, when I'm around you
two. That you ask me what
you should do. It's like we
come home and you say,
"Well should we sell the farm,
or build a house, or what?" I
feel you put the responsibility
on us and it's not our responsibility.

Mom: I think Mike and Marla
feel the same way.

Van: I guess where my anger
comes in is when you use us
to take care of you. When I
was living there and working
there until I was 18, I felt my
contract was clear. I lived in
your house and worked for
you. After 18, I don't want to
work for you or take care of
you. I don't want responsibility for your life. I feel you
keep putting that out to me.
Like the new house that

you can't quite get built. It's like you need us to come in and talk to the Board of Supervisors for you. I'm sure I could have all the regulations together for you in a week. I could do that for you and I'm not going to do it! I want you two to do it. You build your own house! That's real important.

I think you don't get going on the house because then you'd have to sit in it together. I don't think you want to face each other. I'm tired of being a distraction to what you're going to do with each other when you don't have us kids to yell at!

Mom: Well, I suppose that's true. It started so many years ago. Dad would say, "OK, Mom, you go to church with the kids. You go to the wedding with the kids." He never went with me. So he sent the kids with me as substitutes.

After this impassioned complaint by her daughter, Mom moved to avoid any responsibility. She tried to retreat behind the familiar safety of volunteering Dad up as the real villain. This would leave her as a mere victim.

My effort here is to contaminate the comfort of this

position. I want the family to
see this as a partnership
between Mom and Dad, not
as a victim/villain dance
routine.

Carl: Did you ever figure out
what trick you used to make
him do that?

Mom: I don't know. I didn't
think that it was . . . he just
didn't want to go along. I
don't know why.

Carl: Oh, I think you ought to
take 50% of the credit. I don't
think you should give him all
the credit.

I want Mom to have the
opportunity to face her full
participation. Until she does,
she's powerless to change.

The idea of taking equal credit for marital struggles or, for
that matter, successes is one that receives a tremendous amount
of lip service, but very little real-world backing. When put to
the test, this position quickly crumbles. This makes it a potentially treacherous posture. Saying one thing and acting in another fashion sows the seeds of self deceit.

As I see it, the confusion enters when we tabulate events and
interactions over a period of time, then tally them up to see
who really was the villain, and who the victim. The lists of
unacceptable behaviors are typically unbalanced. This is because what is noted are observable behaviors rather than the
full cycle of an interactive sequence. We record the behavior
without noting the "non-response" response of the spouse that
completes the cycle. When you see the "fact" of the full interac-

tive sequence, the columns even out. Every action is shared, even if the sharing is covert.

Van: I guess the other part where I feel angry is that you don't give me the support I need to solve some of my problems. I feel that I can't really use you as a resource or as a parent.

Carl: Wait a cottonpicking minute! You mean you want to be an adult and not take care of them and to be a child so they can take care of you? Make up your cottonpicking mind. Do you want to be 7 or 18?

Here I'm trying to contaminate what seemed to me an overattachment to the wish world of a young child. I want Vanessa to really struggle with the belief that her parents have the responsibility of making her life more whole. While it's normal to want support and care from your parents, the intensity of her feelings was problematic. This keeps her young.

Van: Well, I want to be an adult but I don't want to take care of them. I also want some support from them.

I feel . . . how can I say
it . . . ?

Carl: You can't say it. You've
already said it.

Van: That I want to be both
an adult and a child?

Carl: Sure! You want them to
take care of you but you don't
want to pay the debt. If you're
going to be their child and
have them take care of you,
you ought to let them be your
child and you take care of
them.

Van: Well, I don't want to do
either. I want to get out of
that.

Carl: Well . . . Good luck!

After she ponders an either/or
proposal, I try to return to
the fact that the yoked desires
to belong and individuate are
lifelong companions.

This is how it has to be! While it carries a paradoxical feel,
it's really not so tricky. We all carry with us throughout life the
desire to be taken care of, nurtured, and adored. I don't know
anyone who has really outgrown it. Parallel to this need is the
desire to be independent, self-sufficient, and autonomous.
That is, to feel that we're in charge of our own living and not
overly influenced or controlled by others. No one ever gets over
this, or really achieves it either.

So the two forces are in place for an active interplay over the
course of life. We find many forums in which to enact this
struggle. The solution is not to hope for a clear-cut winner but

rather to blend these needs in a complementary fashion. Your ultimate capacity to be an autonomous, self-sufficient person is directly linked to your capacity to be a part of and to really belong to others. Belonging and individuation are intertwined. They are not antagonistic concepts; they operate in symmetry. The more you have of one, the more you have access to the other. They enhance rather than oppose each other. This yin/yang type of relationship points to integration as the ultimate goal.

As is the case with much of our emotional living, we are influenced, perhaps hypnotized, by the way our parents deal with these universal issues. The willingness to bring them out into the open can serve to demystify the power of this influence. By struggling with the individuation-belonging issue out loud, the whole family has the opportunity to see it in a different light. They can begin to make some decisions based on what they really want from life, not merely based on the subtle music playing in their heads.

Van: In front of people I feel shy. I feel like a little girl.

Carl: Don't you feel like a little girl anyway?

Van: Oh, I do! I do!

Carl: I assume that's part of your ambivalence . . . that you feel like a little girl.

Here I'm attempting to help Vanessa face directly her feelings of being childlike. These feelings don't settle well with her desire to be independent.

Van: Yes, I do. That comes up with my job, and with lovers too. That little girl part

greatly interferes with my
life.

Carl: Well, it's also helpful. It's
true in the animal kingdom as
well. When the female bird is
in heat, she acts like a baby
bird. It attracts the male that
way. A lot of women have
learned that trick, . . to play
helpless. Look at your mother.
I suspect she played helpless
and that's why he grabbed her.
He thought he could get away
with pushing her around. It's
worked pretty well!

Now, in a more pronounced
way, the power of her helplessness is revealed. As she
struggles against the notion of
seducing males via a weakness
ploy, she is faced with her
own relationship suffering. If
she is to deviate from the
methods of her mother, she
first needs to face the price to
be paid.

Van: Well, that may be good
for attracting someone, but
it's not good for a relationship!

Carl: Well . . .

Van: Well, for me . . .

Carl: So suffer!

With this comment I'm telling
her there may be no solution
to find. That the real issue
may be how to better tolerate
the pain. To accept pain as a

partner in life, not to try to avoid it.

Van: . . . or fight it out.

Carl: . . . or both! If you fight it out, you're going to be lonesome. You see, Mom is enslaved, but she's not lonesome. You can fight it out and be independent and not marry anyone, but then you'll be awful lonesome.

Mom: That's right.

Carl: So you can take your pick. You've got to pay the piper and it's a high price either way.

Mom: It's hard to be alone.

Carl: You shouldn't get married unless you're willing to be alone.

(*laughter*)

This seemingly flippant ending comment draws attention to the impossibility of having your marital cake and eating it too. It is meant to contaminate the fantasy that marriage is a cure for loneliness. It often intensifies it!

This exchange touches on the basic human struggle of wanting to be grown up, while not wanting to be lonely. The complicating part is the universal delusion that we can have both all the time. Perhaps we'll someday accept the notion that the struggle is a dialectic to be lived, not solved. It is central to our existence.

Our culture's complex view of marriage may represent the most advanced form of this dilemma. As Helmuth Kaiser (1965) so aptly put it, we enter into marriage with a fully developed "delusion of fusion." This represents a revisiting of the symbiosis experienced as infants with Mother. An expectation that once the marital vows are properly exchanged, our lives will be made whole, our voids filled, and our needs met. While this may, in fact, occur for a limited time, it is typically tarnished before the morning after arrives. What's especially appealing about this delusion is the conviction that not only will the fusion be wonderful, but after the fusion, you'll be in charge. Closeness is expected, with the assumption that life will precisely follow your fantasized script. It's unfortunate that spouses tend to be so imperfect. Ultimately, the need to rub up against each other and contaminate the fantasies must emerge if intimacy is sought.

A first step in transcending this "delusion of fusion" is to become more of a person yourself. The basic ingredients of a whole person "she" and a whole person "he" are necessary for the creation of a "we" that can approach intimacy. Lacking a "he" and a "she" of some maturity, the process of trying to become a "we" is fraught with confusion, misunderstanding, and disappointment.

In leaving Vanessa with, "You shouldn't get married unless you're willing to be alone," I'm trying to contaminate her "*and they lived happily ever after*" fantasy. Our culture holds precious the fantasy that marriage is an end to be achieved, not a process journey to be embarked upon. It's funny how the rules and maneuvers of courting rarely endure the realities of married life.

While the exchange in this vignette is largely between Vanessa and me, Mother's comment reveals her recognition of the pattern under discussion. In a backdoor way, the choice made by her and John is underscored and viewed as a volitional act, not as an accident. The typical explanation used by so many married couples, that of "temporary insanity," to account for their mate selection has been debunked.

This public exchange regarding the dynamics of mate selection opens the way for all of the family members to think more clearly. They can now examine, fantasize, and actively pursue the types of relationships they desire. By hearing these politics in clear language, the children may escape the family patterning of falling into identical dynamics in their own mate selection. They may also be less prone to the other reaction of overcompensating for perceived problems in their parents' marriage by unconsciously seeking the opposite type of person. This, of course, often turns out to be a thinly disguised carbon copy of the very pattern they were determined to avoid. As for the parents, their dynamics will never be quite the same now that their dance has been exposed. They may choose to repeat the steps, but may never fully recover the same level of comfort and nonchalance as they dance.

But well-established patterns die hard. Here Mom cites another example of how she was left alone with the kids. There is a difference, though. Here she introduces the notion that she could have tried something more severe. While she may have mentioned "forcing him at gunpoint" in a whimsical fashion, or with no idea of really doing it, I opted to take it seriously. I wanted to build on her fantasy production.

Mom: We were never together that much because the kids were always there. They went all over with me. A couple of times I said, "You know, John, you should go to the laundromat." Of course, I didn't force him at gunpoint, like I should have.

Carl: Do you have a gun? You could get a little Italian

Beretta. They're very small
and you could carry one in
your pocketbook. The .25
caliber is better than the .22.

Building on Mom's idea of
forcing Dad to participate at
gunpoint is exciting. It adds
to the foundation of Mom
deciding to be a person.

Mom: The last time I even
said to him . . .

Carl: You could get an electric
cattle prod. Do you know
about them?

Mom: Yes.

Carl: They're very nice! Then
every time you wanted him to
go someplace with you, you
could say, "Please, John,
zzzzzzzt!

Mom: He always says, "I'm
tired and I'm going to bed!"

Carl: But he'll change. I can
hear him now: "I'm tired. I
have to go to bed
now . . . AAAAAAAIIIII!"

Mom: Sure he can change.

Carl: "OK. Let's go to the
dance. I'll go! Don't zap me
again!"

Our metaphoric discussion
moves closer to home with an
implement farmers know
about. This talk may awaken

Dad. Extending the fantasy through an actual discussion of what it would look like adds a reality component.

As the session continues, the issue of Vanessa and boyfriends returns. Her way of attracting men by being a little girl resurfaces. She mentions picking men who like that little girl image.

Carl: So now you know how to get one if you need one.

Van: Just be a 7-year-old.

(*laughter*)

Carl: He can get you a big dolly at the circus.

By concretizing the little girl side of her ambivalence, I'm hoping she'll be free to move.

Van: Jesus! I feel this is just getting ridiculous!

Carl: Well, it's already ridiculous. I'm just trying to make it a little more picturesque!

(*laughter*)

I want to keep them in charge of their own living. Her protest of this being ridiculous is merely another way of asking me to take over. I decline the request.

Van: I know! You're picking up on it. I get into this real child role with men. I want them to take care of and mother me. I want to put

those needs here with my
parents, but I see it's not
appropriate here either.

Carl: Well, it may be appropriate but if you hire her, you've
got to pay her.

Van: Right! The full exchange.

Mar: Maybe your guru gave
without wanting something
back.

Van: Yes.

Carl: What do you mean? He
wants your soul, doesn't he?

Van: Oh yes! Right!

(*laughter*)

I've given away my soul!

Again, debunking the belief
that someone else can do it
for you is vital. Turning your
life over to a guru may be
temporarily reassuring, but
you must get it back before
you can be a real person.

As the session nears an end, Dad decides to get involved in a
more personal way. As noted earlier, the sense of emerging
openness in the family now makes it safe for Dad to venture
forth. Here he asks if miscarriages could be related to the
spraying of herbicides to kill weeds. He expressed considerable
guilt about the four miscarriages in the family, associating each
with a weed spraying.

Carl: Did you ever tell Mom
about this before? About your
feeling guilty about this?

Mom: No.

Dad: Well, we discussed how I didn't like to use the spray.

Carl: (*to Mom*)
He may end up being a human being if you're not careful. Here he's been living with all this guilt for years and told no one. Not you or any of the kids. Did any of you know?

Dor: No.

Carl: Why don't you tell people things? Just stupid?

Dad: Could be. Sometimes I don't think about it until it's too late.

Carl: I don't mean the facts. I mean you telling about your suffering. They tell you. Why shouldn't you tell them?

Rather than merely keeping others out, Dad's protective shell is clearly a way of containing his own pain. I'm suggesting a way of relieving the pressure.

While this came out in a slightly disguised form, the fact of Dad bringing his own emotional inner life before the family is impressive. After years of keeping the lid on the guilt and terror he felt for possibly causing four miscarriages, he is seeking relief. His decision to become more personal and to take more of a risk is testimony to the family's growth potential.

This is a typical phenomenon in the process of family therapy. As the sessions progress and the therapeutic set becomes established, the various family members develop enough comfort and courage to become more personal. As it becomes clear that pain is not really the enemy and that struggles don't result in annihilation, the human side emerges.

I wanted to underscore the risk Dad took, making sure it didn't go unnoticed. It's a rare occurrence in the family and may lead to a pathway of continued change. My effort is to support this sort of shift by teasing Dad about being at risk for developing into a human being. It wouldn't pay to be too gushy or flowery with him. I also want the kids to realize that perhaps he's more complicated than just the veneer of a distant dad. While he's played that role for years, he need not be doomed to it. I want them to consider the possibility that he's a person, complete with feelings, fears, and weaknesses, not just a stoic bully.

Calling him stupid is another way of challenging the role, while encouraging the person to step forward. I want to address him in a way that catches his attention. Calling a man stupid is a good way. Then I want to suggest another way of being that may not be so stupid. That is, to talk with the family about his inner world. It's a kind of reframe. Where previously he operated as if sharing his emotional life was stupid, I now want to flip it so that containing all of his pain is stupid. When it comes from another man, he may be able to consider it.

His silence over the years is of course not only a function of his personality. The family must also be considered. Perhaps no one really wanted to know that side of him. Maybe he was forced into isolation, or at least scared away. A teddy bear kind of daddy-husband may have been too threatening.

8
Caring Revisited

One of the most complex aspects of being a therapist is to care in a way that is growth enhancing, rather than merely informative, or even destructive. Most of us enter this business with the innate capacity to be empathic and concerned. We're good at being nurturing in terms of the traditional notions of offering support and being understanding. This capacity is central to our role. Without it we can do nothing. In order to be helpful, we do need to be able to feel the pain of our clients and to appreciate their struggles. While this is essential, it's not enough! If this type of nurturance is all we have to offer, the therapeutic relationship will be severely limited. As in any other type of relationship, depth or intimacy can grow only as the result of real exchange and real struggle.

In order to be truly caring, you must also develop the capacity to be confrontive. You need to be willing to challenge people to face issues they'd prefer to not acknowledge. When I push a family or family member to take a position, I'm conveying that I do care. I'm letting them know that I know better than to treat them like a nobody. Of course, pure confrontation without nurturing is rarely of much value either. Being sadistic and hiding it behind a self-righteous sense of professionalism is a dirty trick.

True caring requires a blending of nurturance and confrontation, an integration of love and hate as paired concepts. They're complementary by nature, not antagonistic. As your capacity to love increases, so does your freedom to hate. Your caring is the ingredient that allows confrontation to be useful rather than abusive. Confrontation without caring is mere sadism.

Another aspect of caring relates to the breadth of emotions you feel about your clients. The diversity of feelings typically

173

increases with time. As we interact over time, the emotional richness expands. Again, the full spectrum, from love to hate, is relevant. Clients can sense a therapist's feelings about them and typically respond accordingly.

The other crucial component to the whole issue of caring is to be respectful of the resources and capabilities of our clients. Part of this is to be cognizant of your own limitations as a therapist. While families may approach us in the midst of a crisis, they are by no means helpless. By virtue of their inter-connectedness, they have tremendous resources to tap. The saying, "One kiss from Mother is worth a thousand by a thera-pist," is true. They have the potential to be helpful to one another, to be growth inspiring. By comparison, our potency is rather weak.

In an odd sort of way, our greatest power or impact stems directly from our capacity to be real. To the extent that we are real with them, they will learn to be real with us. Part of this means never really betraying yourself. Once it's clear to you that you remain the center of your living, they'll begin to be-come their own center. Colluding in a joint delusion that you'll be just the god they'll need serves no one well. It's doomed to bitterness and resentment. I often tell families, "Listen, I'm not really in this for you. I'm here for me and what I can get out of it." I want them to face their own power and responsibility. As we rejoin the family, the issue of my caring and their resources becomes focal.

The third day of the consultation marked the arrival of Gail and Mike, the two missing siblings. With the full nuclear fami-ly now convened, the air was filled with a renewed sense of apprehension and uncertainty. While some of this is a natural consequence of having the full team present, some resulted from the change in our set. In a sense, Mike and Gail were now intruders on an already established process with the original subsystem. While their birthrights as full-fledged family mem-bers weren't in question, their position in the therapeutic su-prasystem was unclear.

Carl: I don't know how to get you into this, Mike. Did they fill you in?

Mike: Not really. You could all just continue on.

Carl: Well, if I do that you're in trouble. My feeling is that everybody in the family is equally crazy. We tried to exteriorize it in everybody. I know that you love diesels and that you're crazy enough to take the farm over from the old man. That's pretty crazy because he'll be looking down your back forever to see what you're doing with "his" farm.

So maybe you could share some of your craziness.

Mike: What do you want me to show?

Carl: I don't know. I guess how crazy you can be . . . or how crazy you used to be. Like when you thought you'd run your own life, instead of having the family run it for you.

Mike: I don't know, I haven't changed that much.

Carl: What are you going to do when the old man moves to the new house and he's not

there to bug you? Get a wife?
I guess you could use your
sister?

Mike: I don't know. Maybe
have other people move in.
Guys I know.

Carl: Now that's an idea! You
could start a commune for
men. You'd have to have a
good cook.

Mike: Yes. Someone who
could really help.

Carl: You could put an ad in
one of the homosexual journals
for a male cook.

Mike: I'm not looking for that!
I'd call friends I know.

It's always an odd business, trying to get someone caught up
with an already established set. Mike is understandably cau-
tious and not wanting to expose too much of himself. But it's
not just the awkwardness of the situation, it's also his personal
style. He seems to prefer to get his bearings before taking a
chance. This may reflect his feelings about what's safe to do in
the family.

We're down to the final day, however, and there's not enough
time for a leisurely entry. As with the other family members, he
too needed to be initiated. When he backed away from my
overt invitation to be self-revealing, I returned to the formula
the family previously revealed, that of sexuality. When I asked
him about getting a wife and he responded with the idea of
having guys move in, I responded automatically. The com-

ment of an ad in a homosexual journal was reflexive, not planned.

Having made this effort and trusting that Mike was at least minimally involved, I turned to Gail. Being aware of her role in the family as a designated scapegoat, I moved to challenge that status.

Carl: You know one of the things we talked about, Gail, was how much of a sucker Mother is. Apparently, she's a patsy for anybody in the family. I wondered if you were trying to be the family patsy so she wouldn't have to be?

Gail: I don't know if I fit into the role of a patsy. I just want to be myself . . . not necessarily like my mother.

Carl: Well, she hasn't had any chance to be herself, so you better not be like her!

Gail: Well, I don't think I'm like her in that sense. I think I'm myself. I want to be myself.

Carl: Do you think there's any chance you'll make it?

Gail: I hope so.

Carl: That wasn't an answer! You fooled me. Do you think

there's any chance you'll make
it?

Gail: I want to.

Carl: That's another non-
answer! Do you think you
will?

Gail: Yes.

Carl: You think you will?
That's nice. It's going to take
an awful lot of guts!

Here Gail is being non-
committal and vague. I
pushed her to give a definite
response, thereby abandoning
her nobody posture and
moving towards personhood.
This, of course, is also aimed
at Mom.

Carl: Who are you going to
have to fight off?

Gail: Well . . . I don't have to
fight off anybody, really. I just
have to cope with myself. I
have to learn to do things by
myself.

Carl: You know, I don't believe
that! You're going to have to
learn to fight them off if
you're ever going to make it
to being a person, instead of
the family Christ!

I'm now pushing harder on the family-wide issue of being
nonpersons. The freedom and courage to struggle with and

challenge each other is crucial. I'll model it and push them to adopt that style. Perhaps they'll be able to take the risk.

Gail's arrival allows this issue to be more poignantly emphasized. Her fear of being a person is clear and the whole family tends to see her as being nonfunctional. Through my struggling overtly with her, the issues are more clearly raised. This might force all of the family members to look at themselves more honestly.

As we rejoin the session, this struggle continues.

Carl: If you stayed in diapers I think Mom would be great. She wouldn't have to notice that she was getting older. But if you ever try to be a person, instead of a baby for her . . .

Gail: I'm trying! I think it's an identity that has to come over the years.

Carl: That's one of the things that bothers me. Don't say you're trying! Trying doesn't help! It only helps if you make it. It's like saying you're trying to make money. It only matters if you make it. You may have to be as mean as hell to make it. Have you ever learned to be mean?

My rather direct assault on her nonperson status is for real. I fear that she has sacrificed her own personhood in order to save the family. My probes are aimed at

helping her take her own life
more seriously. This may help
her stand up for herself and
not be the family patsy.

Gail: Oh, that's another good
one! I'm basically too good to
be mean!

Carl: That's what I'm worried
about. That's how Mother is.
She's too good to even get in
Heaven. I don't think they
could stand her. God would
be embarrassed.

Gail: She is a good woman.

Carl: It's terrible! It's insulting! She ought to be ashamed
of herself. It means she's not a
person, just a thing.

I'm interested in contaminating
the belief that being a passive
victim is an adequate definition
of being a person. I want to
point to the dehumanizing
element of it. Above all, my
intent is to have them see more
clearly the gruesome price
they're paying.

Gail: She is a person.

Carl: I didn't see any evidence
of it! All I saw was her pain
and suffering and emptiness.
I don't even believe her story
about the old man. I think
she did it to him. She made

him push her around, so she could be a nobody and blame him for it. It sounds like you're doing the same thing.

Gail: No. I'm not exactly like her.

Carl: You're younger, huh?

(*laughter*)

Again, the other side of the coin is revealed. Mother's role as victim is now portrayed as being of her own construction. Dad is framed as her accomplice. He is there to forever bear the weight of her blame.

Carl: Do you ever get mean inside? You know, like you'd like to kill the whole gang?

(*pause*)

One of my kids, when she was 10, woke up one night crying. She said she had a bad dream and had to kill the whole family.

Gail: That sounds like a nightmare!

Carl: Well, it was a nightmare. She's never remembered it. I have because I was worried that she'd shoot me the next day.

You've got to learn to be murderous! You've got to be able to feel like killing people inside of yourself in order to get to be a person. Otherwise you'll end up being a sucker. Mother has never had the courage to even want to kill anybody, unless it was me.

If you were going to kill me, how would you do it?

(*laughter*)

Put ground glass in my soup?

Dor: Maybe she'd drown you in her dishpan.

Mike: Pour hot water on you!

Carl: Or with boiling grease!

Dor: There's plenty of lard around.

By sharing a fragment of my own life concerning a murderous impulse manifested in a dream, I'm normalizing the existence of such impulses. If they occur in my life, of course they're normal. Perhaps this will free them to also be more real.

From the previous effort to normalize murderous impulses, I'm now trying to have the family face them in the here and now. I want them to recognize their humanness. While Mother didn't respond directly, the children happily participated in the murderous fantasy. This is a positive sign.

*   *   *   *   *

Ques: Carl, I don't understand. What was all the emphasis on violence and murderous impulses about? Worse yet, why did you ask the mother to talk about how she would think of killing you? That just seems crazy!

Carl: Well, let me go one step further. We were talking earlier about the sexuality and how you could expose it and thus make their inner fantasies less frightening. This is the same thing. The only thing that's more important in the world than sex is death! And we're all potentially suicidal and homicidal. As Camus (1955) so nicely put it, "You can't ask any other questions until you've decided whether it's worthwhile to live."

So I assume that this . . . Gail has indicated very nicely that she's become a nonperson. She's done this to keep Mother's arthritis from getting worse, to keep her from facing the fact that she's growing old, to keep her from feeling so horrible about her marriage, etc. I'm accusing her of wasting her life! Of expressing her love in a way that she doesn't need to. I'm saying that she doesn't need to stay in diapers. That the only way she's going to get over that is to learn how to be dangerous, to be violent, to be mean, to be murderous!

Now you can only go so far with that in the absurdity and teasing. Then I flip to Mother because I assume Gail could learn meanness only if Mother were mean. So far Mother has not been courageous enough to be mean. So I offer her the possibility that she could hate me because I'm a nonperson. I ask, how would she kill me if she decided to? Leaving the "if" in makes it possible for her to have fantasies. It's seeding the unconscious, as I sometimes call it. I drop in things that are ridiculous, but that can form a symbolic experience that later becomes critically significant. Then maybe she can talk about murdering me.

Ques: But isn't that dangerous? Isn't it dangerous to encourage her to fantasize about something that she might be compelled to act on?

Carl: It's the other way around! It's not the talking about it that makes it dangerous. Talking about sex doesn't make it dangerous. It's making believe that it's not important that's dangerous. It's telling your daughter, "I hope you have a good time tonight. I'll wait up for you," instead of saying, "Don't forget! As soon as you leave the house, it's your responsibility whether you get pregnant or not, not mine!"

You face the reality in their fantasy and thus detumesce the reality of their life. You cannot make believe that nothing is there. We're all murderous!

*   *   *   *   *

As discussed earlier, the universality of the impulse world is a psychological reality that somehow is undervalued and often ignored. Perhaps the best way to rediscover it and become reacquainted with its power is to look within ourselves. Viewing our clients from a once removed vantage point is too distant. If homicidal impulses are universal phenomena, and I believe that they are, then we should be able to find them within ourselves. What does it mean if we don't find them? Does it prove that they don't really exist? Or does it indicate that they exist only in some people, that is, our sick patients? Or could it be that we really dare not look too deeply?

It's crazy to think that you can work with a family and their impulse world if you can't access your own. It's worse than crazy! It's dangerous for all! For the longest time I used to carry around a list of the six people I wanted dead. Then as they died off one by one, the list shrunk. I suppose it's time to make up a new one!

While the previous exchange with the family was clearly addressing a crucial area, I was frustrated at not being able to more fully help them access the subsurface anger. Suddenly an association popped into my head. I hopped up and left the room in search of a set of four batacas (pillow bats). This idea came out of my interaction with the family. It was not premeditated. I returned a few minutes later wielding four batacas, two red and two blue.

Carl: Do you like blue or red?

Gail: I like red.

Carl: We'll give the old man this one. It's kind of broken, like old men's things are apt to be.

(*laughter*)

Again, the family reacted to the sexual innuendo.

Do you want one? How about you? I've only got four. It occurred to me that maybe you could make believe you're doing sweet things while you're batting each other in the head with these soft bats that don't really hurt.

(*Family members are holding the batacas but seem reluctant to use them.*)

You can bang it hard and it still doesn't hurt.

In response to their real difficulty in being open about their anger, I've shifted gears. I was feeling stymied at the level of verbal jousting and hoped the introduction of the batacas would encourage more freedom.

(*Mom softly hits herself with a bataca, as does Marla.*)

Van: It's just like Mom to hit herself with it.

Carl: That's the same thing Marla did.

Mar: I was just testing it out.

Carl: You were just testing it out? I thought yesterday that you had the best chance of developing into a human being. You didn't seem too goodie-goodie.

Mar: That's what I'm told.

Carl: Bang her on the head and see how it works.

(*Dad then lightly hits Mom and she retaliates. She repetitively pounds him in the head, as he lowers his arms and just takes it.*

Throughout this section the kids are screeching and laughing in anxious delight.)

Harder! Harder! Harder!

As Mother got warmed up, she was transformed from a hunched over, defeated woman to an active, aggressive, forceful human being. The batacas served to both intensify and release her inner aggression.

The nicest part of this exchange was the "as if" quality of it. While she was hitting Dad, the bataca was both a make-believe pillow bat and a real baseball bat. After all, it's just play. No it isn't, it's real! It's play! It's real! Play! Real!

Mother and the whole family are learning something about their feelings. They're having the experience that their murderous impulses don't really have to result in murder. With this knowledge, they may be free to express their feelings.

Carl: He's no puppy dog. You've got to do better than that!

Mom: Now you hit me.

(*laughter*)

Carl: She's more of a sucker than he is.

(*Dad removes his glasses.*)

Carl: Now with his glasses off you can go to work on him in earnest. Now you can hit him in the face!

Mom: With this? No. It would hurt him.

Carl: No. It would be good for him. His nose is too big anyway.

As Mom begins to retreat from the surprising outburst of aggression and rage, she tries to back away from what had just transpired. I want to let her know that I saw it and feel it was important. Too important to act like it never happened. By suggesting that

she could be even tougher
and more merciless, I hope to
eliminate the kind of guilt
that leads to cover-ups and
denial.

*   *   *   *   *

Ques: What about this scene with the batacas? It just seems
dangerous! It just seems risky to trigger people to actually act out those kinds of impulses in the real world.

Carl: That's not true. It's the other way around. It's the people
who don't have a chance to play out their violence who
become violent. It's the good boys who are dangerous.
There are also, of course, criminals. I'm not talking
about them. But ordinary people are so afraid of their
own fantasies that if you can help them have their fantasies in a justified, nonterrifying way, then they don't have
to worry about the behavior. It's also been my experience.
I've been doing this for a long, long while and I've never
had any real bad repercussions.

Ques: But what is the message that Mom has as she's pounding
on her husband? Is she thinking that this is play, or does
she think she's really killing him?

Carl: Both! Both! She's experiencing the fantasy of destroying
him, but nothing is going on that's dangerous. She's having the emotional expression of it. It's a kind of psycho-
drama, if you will. It's a way of acting dangerous, because you feel dangerous, but not being dangerous.

Ques: And you don't worry that when she goes home she'll re-
place the bataca with an ax?

Carl: No, I certainly don't. I think it's the other way around. I think it's very possible that the arthritis is a way of not using an ax. The batacas are a better way of not using an ax.

*   *   *   *   *

As the session continued, the family was trying to prod Gail into using the batacas on Dad. She resisted this encouragement. Vanessa then commented on wanting to see Gail really get angry sometime. Gail responded that she sometimes did feel angry with Vanessa. She added that she was currently miffed with her because she was leaving the family immediately following the sessions to travel to New York for a trip. She felt that, since the family rarely convened as a full group, being together should have been a higher priority.

In the midst of this discussion, Dad jumped in with a question about the batacas.

Dad: Is there some game you play with these?

Carl: Yes. Just like the two of you were playing.

Dad: Who's the winner?

Carl: The one who beats the hardest. The one who gives up the first is the loser.

Dor: Go for it, Gail!

Mom: Try it, Gail!

Gail: Well, I don't know.

Van: I'll do it with you.

(*The two sisters stand up, with Vanessa hitting in a normal*

*fashion and Gail barely touching
her.)*

Van: Gail is just tapping me.

Gail: Don't hit too hard.

Van: You're not fragile.

*(As Vanessa hits Gail and Gail
feebly defends herself, the family
cheers the action.)*

Gail: Do you have to sit there
cheering?

Dor: What do you want us to
do?

Van: That was fun!

With the second bataca battle now completed, the family
settled back on the couches. Gail began the discussion.

Gail: I do get angry at times.

Mom: We all do. I get mad at
you sometimes.

Gail: It's all how we cope with
getting angry and with our
emotions.

Carl: What a crock of crap!
Why don't you talk straight,
instead of all that social
garbage? Say what you want
to say! All I hear from you is
this mental health type talk!

(silence)

Again, I'm trying to move her
away from a patient or sick

position and encourage her to be more real.

Carl: Who do you think will be the next Christ in the family if you decide to give up the position?

Gail: The next Christ?

Carl: Yes. Who will go crazy next if you go normal?

Gail: Vanessa.

Carl: I don't know. She may be too silly. I don't know if it would be Marla or Doris.

If you get over being crazy somebody else will need to take a turn.

Here I'm pushing the idea that they are, in fact, interconnected. That the family functions as an interactive unit, with all roles available to all.

Mom: Does every family need to have a scapegoat?

Carl: If the stress is too great. If there is a marriage of convenience and if Mom and Dad aren't having a good time with each other. Then they get the kids in the middle so they can get some cuddling from the kids. It frequently ends up with a victim.

(*silence*)

Van: So is that how Gail got crazy?

Carl: Sure. By being elected.

Van: What if we don't want to have her elected anymore?

Carl: I guess you'll have to vote again. It's not easy to change presidents once they're in office. They do so many things for others. Like letting you hit them and not hitting back.

They need to be clear about the amount of work real change entails. It is not easy.

    As we come to the end of this three-day experience, I give them the opportunity to express any closing thoughts.

Carl: Are there any questions you guys want to ask before we quit?

Van: One thing I noticed in the sessions is there's a lot of sadness, a lot of tears in the family. I just feel like Dad is waiting to die. Sometimes I get concerned about Marla's drinking. Like sometimes you drive too fast and it feels self-destructive. Sometimes I don't know where you are, Gail. I feel you've given up. I feel, Doris and Mike, you haven't given up. You're fighting it. You're pretty stable. Sometimes I just feel

waves of depression and a real
morbid quality to the family.

Mom: Life's always been
pretty heavy.

Carl: Yes. Living is pretty
heavy.

Mom: Yes it is.

Carl: But there's no reason
you can't . . .

Mom: . . . have a little humor.
I tried to put a little humor in
it. Every time I did, Dad cut
it down.

Carl: So you finally gave up
after two years of marriage?

Mom: No. I kept trying.

Carl: Any questions from you,
Mike?

Mike: No. Nothing offhand.

Carl: Gail?

Gail: No.

Carl: Doris?

Dor: Not really.

Carl: Marla?

Mar: No.

Carl: Mom?

Mom: No.

Carl: Dad?

Dad: No.

Carl: I've enjoyed having you
and the chance to get to know
you. I will always think of
you.

The process of ending with a family is an integral part of the therapy process. It's a crucial component in how they see and integrate the therapy into their ongoing experience of living. Like any parent, in the therapist role as a foster parent I'm both sad to see them go and pleased that they're able to venture forth.

I want to convey a message of concern, caring, and interest, while in no way suggesting that I disagree with their choice to terminate. They need to know that I have a certain trust in them. That they can face the world on their own. I also want them to know that while I won't cling to them, I will be available for them should they ever decide to return.

This sort of an ending leaves the responsibility for living where it belongs, right in their collective hands. They need to be steering their own ship. They, of course, can always call when they want to reconvene. I want them to know that I will be available to them.

Like all the others, when they leave I feel abandoned. Having a professional cuddle group is the best way I know to decompress and maintain hope for the future.

9
The Healthy Family
and Normal Pathology

One of the difficulties in working with families lies in trying to determine what is healthy and what isn't. How do we tell the difference between a family functioning in the "normal" range and one mired in "pathology"? While there really aren't any universally recognized criteria, we all have some notions that guide our thinking.

Perhaps the most valid point of entry into these murky waters is to consider our own personal criteria. We all make such judgments of others all the time. No amount of scientific thinking, clinical neutrality, or personal open-mindedness can really do away with this natural human phenomenon. Regardless of our educational history and professional training, the standard we automatically apply reflects our own constellation of personal perspectives, biases, and distortions. We can view others only through the eyes of our own experience.

When I begin with a family, it is most common for me to begin with the father. In doing so, I naturally compare him to my internalized standards for what a father is and what a father does. This composite is strongly self-reflective, moderately tied to my views of my own father and mildly related to other "father" figures I have encountered. This new father under the microscope quite naturally gets good marks for things I like about myself, my father, and the adjunctive father figures I've internalized. Similarly, bad marks accumulate in the same fashion on the opposite side of the spectrum. This instinctive assessment also occurs regarding Mom, the relationship between Mom and Dad, the kids, their mutual relationships, the parent-child relationships, and on and on. This type of personalized evaluation system is at the core of all the judgments and inferences I make about people. Quite naturally, I fit the "them" I encounter into the internal interpersonal template I've developed over the years.

It's not really a planned or conscious process. It just happens! When Mom says something that triggers a memory of my own mother, I automatically assume she means the same thing my mother meant. While it may have little to do with what this mother intended, or how this family takes it, I hear it in the only way I can. The fact that I may be somewhat aware of this process doesn't stop it. We all transfer onto each other all the time. I can experience you only through the me I know. Perhaps the advantage of at least being clear about this is that I've learned to not try to force you to be me. I certainly wouldn't want you to try to make me be you, so I try to return the compliment beforehand. You don't have to experience the world in the way that I do in order for me to consider you "sane."

Family Life

Despite the pervasiveness of this personal factor, there are a number of significant ways to look at and talk about families. First of all, the healthy family is one that is dynamic, not static. It is in a process of continual evolution and change. Health is a perpetual state of "becoming." You never really "get there" or finish the journey. So the healthy family is a system in motion. While you can take a look in a freeze-frame mode, or evaluate a cross-sectional image, you need a sense of the family movement over time to really know about it. At any particular point in time, the picture you take may distort the whole.

When we begin to look at the family in motion, we realize the dance is not random. Like any other social organization, there are rules, policies, and patterns. The rules are typically covert and nonarticulated, often not even in conscious awareness, but they are potent nonetheless. In healthy families, these rules serve as guidelines and are in the service of a growth effort. In pathological families, the rules are used to constrict change and maintain the status quo.

One of the basic components in the structure of a well-functioning family is a clear separation of the generations. It is clear that the parents and the children are not equal in terms of authority and responsibility. The parents are the real backbone of the family, with the children getting their sense of security from the parents' leadership and solidarity. But a healthy separation of the generations is not to be confused with a rigid hierarchical structure. It's not predicated on the idea that the parents exert dominance over the children, but rather on the idea that their strength provides security and safety. It's more of an undercurrent phenomenon. Their strength is sensed but not always overtly displayed.

In the healthy family, the strength of the parents operates in a covert way. Since their strength is clear, they don't have the need to continuously prove it, either to the children or to themselves. They foster an openness regarding play, role experimentation, and role exchanges. The family may live in an "as if" structure, whereby they are all free to exchange roles and functions within the security of the solid understructure.

For example, Dad is secure enough that he doesn't have to win all of his power struggles with his four-year-old son. He doesn't have to retain a rigid pattern of living to feel that he's really the one in charge. He can let little Johnny play daddy and try to cut the meat at the dinner table. Dad may even be able to get into it enough to act out Johnny's role of whining about the vegetables or complaining about the brown rice. For her part, Mom can permit her eight-year-old daughter to give her a backrub when she's feeling poorly, or to fold the wash even though she doesn't do it perfectly. She can give her son the flexibility of choosing when he'll clean his room without becoming rigid. The kids are free to treat Mom special sometimes, without Dad becoming jealous. They can do something nice for Dad without Mom feeling betrayed. This kind of role flexibility doesn't erode a solid structure, it enhances it.

The healthy family can live with changing triangles and fluctuating coalitions without breeding insecurity and jealousy. In fact, having the freedom to experience all of the possible triangle combinations and permutations is an enriching experience. Being free to team up, then to disengage and change partners is vital to establishing healthy boundaries. This also encompasses the need to really separate, to go off and be an individual without feeling guilty about letting go of the family. It's only when you're free to not belong that joining with someone has any meaning. The teaming is then clearly volitional, a matter of choice, not obligation.

This sort of structure offers each family member the experience of being part of a secure and caring whole, while at the same time encouraging independence and self-expression. The togetherness that emerges is then real because it is freely engaged in. Each person is free to leave and then rejoin, separate again and return, ad infinitum. These capacities grow in synchrony, they are not antagonistic concepts. Under these conditions, a certain sense of family loyalty or nationalism arises. They tend to want to be with each other. By being together with the others, each member feels more whole, more complete.

As a healthy family moves through the life cycle, it is free to change, adapt, and grow without fear and apprehension. New circumstances represent an opportunity, not a threat. The inevitable conflicts and problems that arise are dealt with without their losing sight of their undercurrent caring and love. At different times, in different situations, different family members will end up in the role of the scapegoat. This capacity to have and accept rotating scapegoats is more healthy than to live sterilely, hoping no scapegoat emerges. Being a scapegoat is only devastating when the role becomes fixed and rigid. Families that live in a semiphobic world of trying to avoid all pathology typically become victim to it.

Perhaps one of the real hallmarks of a healthy family is the capacity to use crisis to spur growth, rather than allowing it to splinter them. Conflict should rightly be considered the fertilizer of life. While not always fragrant, it's crucial for optimal growth.

Another indicator of family health is room for the intimacy of loving, as well as for the upset of hating. All are free to engage in intense interchange, from a basis of love as well as hate. Emotional issues such as sexuality, religion, child-rearing, etc., can be argued without threatening the continuity and togetherness of the unit. The core is solid enough to not only withstand but also grow from such encounters.

There is also the freedom to acknowledge and embrace the three- or even four-generational family unit. The parents can focus on the old days, with the children being interested. The children can be involved with their grandparents without it evolving into pathological triangling against the parents. The older generation can engage the younger generation without hiding behind a distancing demand for impersonal "respect." They can all look to the future and talk about the next generation without fearing that it takes away from the present. This whole evolving family interchange is viewed as being part of an ever-emerging family culture.

Finally, the healthy family is an open, rather than closed, social organism. Non-family members are incorporated into, rather than extruded from, family life. Friends, neighbors, etc., can enter into the family space and be accepted and enjoyed, not viewed with suspicion. Any family member feels free to bring a friend to the family, without fear that he will be rejected.

As we talk about families, it's important to bear in mind that we are more bound by similarities than separated by differences. That all of the patterns or mechanics that we consider pathological and, therefore, indicators of unhealthy families are also found in every "normal" family. The difference typically lies in intensity, rigidity, and time span rather than in the appearance of these problems.

When you see a family over time, their behavior not only becomes more understandable, but typically makes sense. Their massive interconnectedness, with every action being both a stimulus and a response, keeps the whole system moving in an internally consistent fashion.

Marriage

In talking about the family, it's important to take a moment to specifically focus on the foundation of the family, the marriage.

A healthy marriage really is a blending of two foreign cultures. It's an effort to blend these two cultures into one new culture that is both similar to and yet distinctively different from either of the contributing clans. I've often described the cross-generational politics as two families sending out scapegoats to replicate themselves. Life is then lived to see who wins. The real key to avoiding this sort of ridiculous contest is reaching a transcendent level of living. It's not acceptable to replicate one family or the other. Everybody loses under those conditions. The new couple must be clearly different from either family of origin, while remaining cognizant of the aspects of each worth preserving.

This doesn't happen magically, or even by the exchange of wedding vows. The whole "happily ever after" conspiracy that treats the wedding as the endpoint, rather than as a beginning, is horribly destructive. It leaves both partners anticipating spontaneous and overwhelming love and satisfaction, while ignoring the reality of needing to form a more mature relationship. The sooner you're free of the myth of the perfect match, or the marriage made in Heaven, the sooner you can begin to build towards intimacy.

What happens that makes marriage so special? So special that despite all the struggles and problems it persists as such a marvelously popular institution? While it often begins with the delusional belief of your being made whole, or having your every need met, it rarely stays at this level. The promise of euphoria quickly settles into the reality of day-to-day life. To be able to rise above day-to-day life, you must be able to go beyond a "he" and a "she" and search for the "we" that empowers the marriage. This "we" area is the place of overlap and integration. Finding a workable balance is really the struggle.

Incidentally, it's the loss of this "we" that makes divorce so devastating and infidelity so destructive. Divorce legally declares the "we" to be a nonentity. It declares that the set no longer exists. While it may be a legal fact, I don't believe it happens this way in the world of emotional realities. You can never really get back the emotional investment you placed in a spouse. It remains locked in the "we" set. You can certainly elect to not live together, but you can't decide that what happened didn't happen. You remain part of each other forever. The thing that makes sexual affairs so disastrous is that they not only define the current "we" as being rather unimportant, but also create another "pseudo-we."

Affairs often seem to arise in relationships that have gone dead. The term "stalemate" seems appropriate here. As the mates do in fact become more stale with each other and stagnation sets in, they notice the increasing deadness and aloneness. The idea of trying to find again the kind of excitement that once existed is appealing. While the trade-in fantasy frequently fuels the actual move towards an affair, it often remains relatively superficial. The fantasy of finding that perfect pairing and having joy spontaneously occur is tempting but elusive. Intimacy takes work. It emerges over time via joint struggles and sharing. Marriages either grow together or grow apart. There's no neutral to shift into. While an affair may serve the purpose of kicking up the thermostat and creating some intensity, the cost is typically gruesome. The emotional residual is never really washed away.

The notion of commitment in marriage is also crucial but typically poorly understood. The "till death do us part" pledge ought not be perceived as a life sentence without the possibility of parole. The commitment it really seeks to ensure is one that constitutes an agreement to really try to grow closer, to communicate more honestly, and to put the needs of your spouse on almost equal footing with your own. The idea of commitment is intended to counter the impulse to cut and run at the first sign of disillusion.

204 Dancing with the Family

All healthy marriages experience literally dozens of emotion-al divorces over the course of the years. Whether they last for three minutes, three hours, or three days, the feeling of loss can be overwhelming. To the committed couple, these periods of emotional separation are painful, but they fall short of irrevers-ible despair or hopelessness. They retain a sense of comfort based on their history of being willing and able to work and struggle productively. They "know" they can survive this pain-ful period.

The capacity to deal with differences is one development that greatly stabilizes and enhances the quality of the marriage. When differences are viewed as inherently bad or as something to be eliminated, they cause schism, evoke defensiveness, and lead to estrangement. However, when differences can be viewed as representing opportunities to grow, they become valuable. Our differences are what allow us to expand. The capacity to really engage in a bilateral process of mutual con-tamination is central to a dynamic, rather than static relation-ship. As we rub off on each other, we are enriched. The steps involved in getting to the point of using differences productive-ly go from acknowledging to accepting to respecting to enjoy-ing and, finally, to treasuring them.

Parenting

This kind of growth as a couple is also what prepares us to be successful as parents. The quality of the husband-wife relation-ship is what is drawn upon as the couple makes the shift to becoming Mom and Dad. It's this bond between Mom and Dad that is crucial for the children. They plug directly into the quality of the caring and loving between their parents. Their sense of security or of panic is reflective of the emotional bond between their parents. It's not the child's relationship to Mom that is central, or his relationship to Dad, but rather his rela-tionship to their relationship.

Conversely, the inability of the husband and wife to establish their relationship before becoming Mom and Dad sets the stage for emotional infidelity and cross-generational triangulation. Lacking a caring couples relationship, the husband and wife become easily overloaded when faced with the demands of parenthood. The couple that never worked through the struggle over who "wins" regarding weekend activities, household tasks, the extended families, what television shows to watch, etc., has no hope when kids enter the picture.

The delusion that having a baby will allow a damaged marital relationship to heal is dangerous. Treating the baby as another Christ with the mission of saving the marriage is ridiculous. It typically ends in even deeper schism and more desperation.

The process of evolving from a couple to a family has a number of predictable shifts. The natural mother-infant symbiosis becomes the focal point of affect in the family. If the father has enough maturity to see it and not become jealous, the family is free to move forward. When Dad becomes too resentful, however, or sulks or shouts because his adolescent sexual needs are being infringed upon, the real trouble begins. If he rants and raves, the wife feels in a bind between the neediness of the infant and that of her husband. If he turns elsewhere for closeness, be it his career or tennis or his secretary, his wife feels abandoned. She is left alone with the responsibility for the child. As their distance widens, the pattern of turning away from each other is set.

As life develops and the infant becomes a child, the lack of parental togetherness again becomes painfully apparent. Mom may feel overwhelmed in trying to cope with Johnny alone. Johnny may experience Mom as being overly restrictive and therefore he will rebel. If Dad fails to take a clear position in support of Mom, Johnny knows it's really a form of covert aid to him. He presses on, secure in the knowledge that he's pleasing his father. Again, the issue of parental togetherness is pivotal.

Another common dance is for an overinvolved mother to be

unable to control her daughter. She then enlists the distant
father as a disciplinarian. When Dad resentfully obliges, he is
perceived by Mom as being overly harsh and punitive. This
triggers Mom to come to the defense of her daughter. This
serves to rigidify the pathologic set. The mother-daughter overinvolvement is increased and Dad's distance is reinforced.

10
Which Direction Is Growth?
Three-Year Follow-up

Trying to evaluate the success or failure of family therapy is an elusive and deceptive business. The obvious question of, "Was the therapy successful?" is often quite dangerous. Dangerous because it presumes generally agreed-upon criteria for success. Criteria that are not only clinically valid but also reliably measured and collected. At this point in time, our field is more art than science. Despite this condition, however, each of us must in some way deal with the issue of what works and what doesn't. We all have some idea of what constitutes "success" and what is failure.

It's my conviction that therapy is a process effort directed towards growth. Its basic aim is not symptom elimination or first-order change. We need to move beyond the idea of reductionistic behavioral referents as adequate reflections of "reality." Growth or "success" is more related to the evolving process of the family, to their capacity to be genuinely personal with each other. The idea of "teaching" direct communication skills also seems somewhat misguided. You can't do it well enough to create intimacy.

The process of growth really begins with the family's courage to take the risk of being more personal with each other. It's their willingness to begin the journey, not how clearly mapped out the route is that is essential. A therapist's involvement with a family should not aim at depriving them of their anxiety. It should focus on transforming their anxiety into something useful, something productive. While lowering the family temperature can sometimes avert blow-ups, any premature move away from intensity also deadens the prospect of real growth. In a culture of escalating alienation, a therapist needs to be able to tolerate efforts involving risk and intensity.

While there is a certain appeal to being able to identify

change in terms of concrete behaviors, growth is more of a transcendent process. The gearshift analogy comes to mind. You can do only so much in first gear. Your ultimate speed and the optimal range of functioning for the engine are quite limited. You can certainly operate the vehicle in first, but it's both inefficient and quite restricted. By shifting to second gear at the appropriate time, however, you get better performance and open a broader range of possibilities. This is how I see families. It's my function to help them shift to another level of living. I want to help them access their underutilized abilities and capacities.

An essential component of this shift is to help them see over the top of their pain. To help them recognize and come to appreciate the absurdity of life. I want them to learn to not only tolerate, but also enjoy the anxiety and pain that make living real. The choice often comes down to being numb or experiencing both agony and joy. I want them to be able to consider the experience of living, not to automatically choose sedation. Would you prefer to struggle with your spouse or hide behind the television set? Tough topics can't be avoided. The agreement to shy away from real issues typically creates a setting of coolness and distance.

One way that I try to avoid the trap of becoming too interested in their concrete living is to remain focused on my own experience of life. Even in the therapy room, I try to keep myself at the center of my existence. I remain more dedicated to my effort to expand and grow than to dutifully try to stretch the family. When I try to stretch them, they become elastic and easily snap back to their original shape when I let go. When they take on the task of remolding themselves, the changes have a chance to really take. Part of the problem is that I don't really know how to form them. My efforts to make them take on a particular shape are bound to be contortionistic. When they guide it, however, the new shape will be more naturally pleasing.

While I've abandoned trying to influence the form of their

creation, I do have some strong ideas about the process required to get there. This is the turf I engage them on. We interact about the process of their living, not the concretization of that process.

While it's my interactive process with them that may stimulate the growth, it's their evolving process that is the growth. For example, my teasing Mom about her martyrish, self-victimization may push her to consider changing, but that's not the growth. Growth only occurs when she begins the journey. It's not even necessary that she fully succeed. Maybe the guts to try is all that's required. Getting past the fear of trying may be enough.

But again, I'm not so interested in how they change, or that it follow a particular pattern. I'm more focused on shaking things up to the point that they're free to begin. As people become more free to live, it's typically detectable in the quality of their interpersonal dynamics. There's a sense of spontaneity and openness, a capacity to be different and to accept differences without panic or terror. The need for full family conformity is replaced by an enjoyment of the areas of difference. The ability to laugh at oneself and with each other replaces the cynical laughing at each other.

It's a sense of transcendence. Whereas the events and dilemmas of external reality are sometimes slow to change, the family faces them with less heaviness and dread. The evolving sense of connectedness and freedom serves as a release from the isolation and unreality that burden them.

Whether Johnny still wets the bed or Mom still can't decide on a new career is not the point. If the therapist gets seduced by the model of behavioral change, he becomes their employee and will be controlled by their actions. While they may oblige with temporary shifts in behavior, the therapist is ultimately at their mercy. When they fail to make significant change, the therapist is stuck. The only out is to declare yourself inept, or them resistive.

My effort is to steer clear of this mess entirely. By keeping

myself at the center of my living and protecting my boundaries, a parallel process may begin. As they establish more appropriate boundaries and take responsibility for their own living, their growth begins.

Revisiting the Family

With three years now having passed since the initial sessions,
the family returned for a follow-up session. As we review this
session, keep an eye open for indicators of growth or change
that may have occurred. The follow-up was set up following a
call from Vanessa, who said the family was planning another
reunion. She asked if I would be available to meet with them. I
readily accepted, remembering how enjoyable our earlier visits
had been.

In working through the logistics for the follow-up, Gail re-
quested that it be a double meeting. She wanted the first part to
be an additional therapy session, rather than just serving as a
follow-up to the previous work.

As the family filed in, there was a sense of eagerness and
excitement, but no discernible fear or apprehension. They
looked different. Dad had lost weight and was less rural in
appearance. Vanessa's attire was more subdued, less flamboy-
ant. Gail was more alert and bright-eyed, with considerable
added weight. Mom wore wrist braces for her arthritis.

As we settled in and began to feel each other out, Gail moved
forward. She began reporting on the events of her life since the
previous meetings. She had dramatically reduced her medications. The sluggishness and blunted affect that had been so
prominent were gone. She had managed to move out of an
institutional facility and was living on her own. She was also
employed.

Gail then brought up the topic of her boyfriend struggles. It
was as if she had now really become a full-fledged daughter in
this family; she, too, was having boyfriend troubles! As we pick

up on the conversation, notice the change from the previous sessions.

Carl: Why did you drop your boyfriend?

Gail: He dumped me. He started going out with other girls. I said he could and he did.

Van: But there were other things, too! Like sex and marriage as big things. You didn't want that, so he said goodbye.

Mom: Yes.

Mar: He asked you to marry him, right?

Carl: Did he want one or both? Marriage or just sex?

Gail: Both.

Carl: Well, that's better than one anyway.

Mom: Yes, it is.

Carl: Sometimes these people want marriage and no sex. I saw a couple a few days ago who had been married for one year. They had agreed to marriage because the husband said there would be no sex.

Mar: Oh, come on!

Carl: It turned out what he meant was it was OK to be married but that he was going to be homosexual. It didn't turn out so well.

Have you found another boyfriend yet?

Gail: No! I'm not looking for a man!

Mom: That's right. She's not even looking.

Carl: What's wrong with you? Not looking for a man is ridiculous.

Gail: Well, not now. I'm hanging out with friends. I do want to join a church group. A singles church group!

Mar: Swinging singles in the church.

Carl: Sure! Some of the best boyfriends are captured in church. The first girlfriend I got there was a stodgy old character, though. I'm glad I didn't stick with her.

Van: I've noticed, Gail, that you've been reaching out to Marla and Doris and they've brushed you off. I was also

This story is one of a figure-ground flip. It's a way of playing with the fact that people live in many patterns. The openness of their exchange is telling. There is a new freedom to participate.

getting irritated with you. Now I understand it with the loss of your boyfriend. I just get broken-hearted when I have a break-up with a boyfriend.

Carl: Maybe you two could pimp for each other.

Van: What?

Carl: You know. Pimp for each other. She'll get you a boy-friend and you'll find one for her.

Van: Well, I have a boyfriend now.

Carl: So you don't need help now? Well, you could send her one from where you live. Although I hear they're not so hot there. You could send one via UPS. In a crate.

Mike: C.O.D.

Dor: But you need the right-sized crate.

Carl: Yes. You might need to squish him up.

This is a nice change. Vanessa spontaneously responds in a supportive, empathic fashion. It's personal, with no trace of criticism or disapproval.

Of note here is the air of playfulness. They all seem to enjoy the exchange. They've learned something about playing.

In addition to being more spontaneous concerning topics of low and moderate intensity, they must broach more difficult topics. Previously, the family tended to identify Dad and Gail as the ones with the "real" problems. In the following segment this changes.

One of the hallmarks of a healthy family is the presence of rotating, rather than fixed, scapegoats. It's pathological to try to encapsulate all the pain of the family within the skin of one or two of the members. Pain is part of life, not something to be avoided. The capacity to face and accept pain is an essential element to a balanced life. All family members are entitled to experience their own suffering and to have the opportunity to receive support from the others.

The capacity to face, rather than deny, pain and to do it in the presence of the family reveals an openness and sense of trust that make life more personal and rewarding. Here the conversation focuses on Mom.

Mom: I hate the category of being considered handicapped (*by arthritis*)! My sister says I should get a license with a wheelchair on it so I can park in a handicapped space.

Carl: An unemployed mother.

Mom: Yes. I don't know if I want to be in that category either! Sometimes I don't know where I belong!

Carl: Do you have much pain?

Mom: Well, sure, if I do too much. Especially with my wrists and feet, too.

Mike: Her ankles are so bad.

Dor: Her ankles are very weak. She sprains one every month.

Mom: I have braces.

Carl: You know, I had another crazy feeling. When you talked about not knowing where you belong, I had the feeling you were talking suicide. Do you feel suicidal?

Mom's talk about not knowing where she belongs and her depression over the arthritis left me with a sense of her hopelessness. When directly asked, she was able to let the family know how bad she felt.

As Mike and Doris shared their concern, Mom was more free to continue on.

Mom: Well . . . sometimes.

Carl: Can you call these guys up when you feel like that and say, "Tell me five nice words"?

Mom: You mean the hotline?

Carl: No! To hell with the hotline!

(*laughter*)

Carl: Seriously! When you get lonesome . . . you know you can't talk to this old character, he talks to the cows.

Can you call the gang and say, "I feel bad. I feel depressed!"?

Mom: I don't know (*tearful*).

Van: You can call me, Mom.

Mom: I guess I'd rather keep it to myself. I don't want to burden them with it.

Carl: That's a lot of malarkey, for God's sake. You mothered them for all these years. Why shouldn't they mother you?

If worse comes to worst, you could go to the old man and see if he'd give you a hug. He might not know how to do it, but you could work on it and teach him. He might even get to like it.

Here I'm pushing Mom to transform her internal suicidal impulse into a family issue. If they make it blatantly inter-personal and involving the full family, the hope of change can grow.

Perhaps at its most basic level, suicide is an effort to have your biological organism come into congruence with your emotional world. The belief that no one really cares about you is then the bullet to do the job. But when this fantasy is exposed to the family reality, the isolation can end and the relationships rekindle.

Mom: He always runs away.

Carl: Of course! Men are all supposed to be afraid of closeness. We're all ridiculous, every damn one of us!

Dor: I wish you would call me. Sometimes you call me and I think, "Boy, this is such a surprise!"

Mom: But I don't have enough money to call.

Dor: Who cares about the money? We'll deal with that later. What matters is how you're feeling. If you're lonely and feeling sad, I want to talk to you about it!

This sort of reaching out can be lifesaving. The undercurrent caring has begun to surface. This may serve to counteract the pain of chronic isolation.

*   *   *   *   *

Ques: Carl, in this segment what helped you know that she was feeling suicidal? It wasn't really that apparent.

Carl: I don't really know. A lot of these things are clinical hunches. I don't know where they come from.

There was a hint in there when I said, "You're an unemployed mother," and she said, "I don't like that either," meaning there's never been anything she really wanted to be. That to me is a suicidal statement.

Ques: You know, suicide is a serious business. You succeed once and it's over. In this situation, did you ever think of medicating or hospitalizing her? Did you consider the more standard ways of dealing with someone you may really be worried about?

Carl: Well, if she were actively and deliberately and operationally suicidal . . . I don't think that's true. I think she's like a chronic alcoholic. She's involved in a gradually invading type of self-destruction. Like the daughter who became a nobody. She's been a nobody for so long that death will just catch up. One of the ways of committing suicide is to keep on living. I don't see her as dangerously suicidal. Were she dangerously suicidal and I convinced that she was dangerous, I would talk much more openly about it. I would involve all of them, assuming that she will not be dangerously suicidal unless there's somebody else in the family who wants her dead. The obvious person would be the husband.

Ques: Well, that's kind of a strange idea. You mean, if mother is feeling suicidal, it's because someone else wants her to be dead?

Carl: Of course! Of course! Suicide is like anything else. All of these things are interpersonal. I really believe in systems! I don't believe individuals operate as units. I think they operate only as part of larger units.

Ques: Couldn't she just be feeling desperately lonely?

Carl: Of course! That means he doesn't want her. That means he wants her out of the way. Then he could dance with anybody he wanted.

That's the way I think about it. This is a subclinical suicide, this thing we're talking about now. Were she really suicidal, I would make the family be her hospital.

Ques: I don't understand! How would you do that?

Carl: I'd make them responsible for her being suicidal. Our task would be to find out why this family wants her dead. Who is it that's leading the pack? What would happen if she died? If she committed suicide, who would cry? Would Father be willing to leave his tractor and go to the funeral? Would the kids, would Vanessa be willing to come in for her mother's funeral? Who would cry the longest? I would ask all these questions of Mother. I would force her into extending the fantasy past her death. This contaminates the fantasy that makes suicide possible.

It's like that famous story about the policeman who was trying to talk a man down off a bridge. An actual story! The man was not interested in all this talk. Finally, the policeman couldn't stand it anymore, so he drew his gun and said, "You son of a bitch, if you jump I'll shoot you!" So the man came down. Now that's real psychotherapy! He broke the fantasy that this man had of what would happen if he died. He blasted it wide open! That's what I like to do. That's what I think is useful and important.

Medication just covers it. Just like going to sleep is one way to get over being in a fight with your wife, but it doesn't help much. It just covers it. You wake up the next morning and make believe nothing happened.

*   *   *   *   *

As we continued on, we stayed with the topic of suicide. I moved to add another interactive vector by talking with Mom regarding how Dad would handle it if she did kill herself.

Carl: Do you know what would happen to him if you committed suicide?

Mom: No.

Carl: I'll tell you. I bet he'd fade out and die within six months.

Mom: I don't know.

Carl: I have this fantasy about myself if my wife died. I think I'd disappear into the woods. I don't know how long it would take before I'd be able to come back. I don't believe I'd really kill myself, but I'd be in a bad state.

Here I'm broadening the spectrum of suicide to also encompass Dad. I'm telling him that the guilt he experiences over the miscarriages, etc., would visit again.

This also highlights his undercurrent dependency on her and debunks the myth that he would just dance his way into the heart of a younger woman.

Leaving them with my fantasy about me leaves them with little to rebel against.

Mom: What about if he would die first? I'd really feel terrible, too.

Carl: Sure.

Mom: I couldn't handle it.

Carl: Sure. It might cure your arthritis, but you'd damn sure be depressed and lonesome as hell.

Do you ever write these characters and tell them about your loneliness by letter?

Dor: No! She only sends

newsy letters. She won't talk about herself.

Carl: So you run away just like he does!

Mom: Yes.

Carl: I don't think you should run away from your own kids. Do you feel it would add to their burden if you told them?

Mom: There's no reason I'm so depressed. I'm just lonesome.

Carl: Sure. You're lonely for the farm and for five kids and a whole past that you don't have anymore.

The key here is to openly challenge Mom's martyrish position of having nothing to be depressed over. I want her to realize that she's hiding from her family under the guise of not burdening them.

I end this with a clear reminder of what Mom has lost. Now the whole family is aware of her pain.

The discussion briefly turns to the concrete realities of life on the farm. They talk of how Dad still works on the farm with Mike and how Mom frequently comes by to help out too. It's clear that Mike is in frequent contact with his parents.

Here Vanessa decides to question her brother, thereby challenging the family belief that men aren't human beings. She's asking if he really has been oblivious to Mom's pain, or if he merely acts that way.

Van: You see Mike about every day, right, Mom?

Mom: Yes.

Mike: Every other day for sure.

Dad: Nobody has time.

Van: Mike, did you know
Mom was feeling so lonely?
Could you pick it up over the
last few months?

Mike: Somewhat . . . but . . . you
know, I don't have the time
either! (*Mike breaks into tears.*)

Carl: You're like Dad. Always
working on the goddamned
farm.

(*The family cries.*)

What a nice indicator of
change. Now one of the men
can own his pain and dare to
express it via tears. This is
growth! Mike is no longer
locked into the family myth
that men are affectless.

Mike: There's never no time!

Van: So you don't have time to
visit with Mom?

Mom: He visits with me a lot.
We don't know what to do
except to work.

The family's increased freedom to face their pain and to be
involved with each other is impressive. The other side of the
coin is their increased playfulness and capacity to laugh. This
emerging sense of openness is central to growth.

As the session continued, I more directly questioned the family regarding the aftereffects of our previous sessions. As is often my style, I opted to begin with Dad. I wanted him to take a position.

Carl: So this is my party. So I can get the story of what those six interviews we had resulted in. To get some idea of what they did to the family.

How about you, Dad? Can you say something about what the experience was to you?

Dad: Well . . . it was enlightening to get a little closer insight into the family. What it should mean to you and what you should mean to them.

Since our last meeting, not today but before, I built a retirement home.

I feel good that I could build this house. Mainly for Marie because it's convenient and cozy and handy.

Dad, too, has become more people-oriented. He is more aware of the interpersonal component of living.

Mom: It is nice to come home to.

Dad: I wasn't a real good husband, but I figured that's what I could contribute.

(*laughter*)   This is testimony to the
                               increasing intimacy in the
                               family. While the mode of
                               expression may be lacking in
                               terms of verbal communica-
                               tion, it is real.
                                  Dad's capacity to label the
                               housebuilding as an attempt
                               to be a better husband is
                               impressive. It may lead to
                               even more closeness over
                               time.

At this point there was an extended discussion about life on
the farm. As is typical, this part of the conversation focused on
work and projects to be completed. Dad was the central figure
in this talk, with the women remaining quite peripheral. While
the facts of this talk were quite similar to those of three years
earlier, there was an interesting difference that was powerfully
obvious. There was no sense of anger, rage, or resentment on
the part of the women. If anything, they seemed to be somewhat interested and to enjoy it.

As I look back, it seems clear enough. As Dad's capacity to
be present in the family has increased, they've become more
able to see him as a person, not just as an uncaring impediment
to family intimacy. Now when he engages in farm talk, they can
see it as his way of coping with the world, rather than as
something he is doing against them.

As this conversation ended, I turned to Mom.

Carl: It was nice this morning
that you could cry about your
suicidal impulses. That was
quite impressive and unusual-
ly flexible. Most people are
much more rigid. When you

ask about suicide, they say, "Oh no! Not me! I've never had a suicidal thought in my life!"

Mom: I wouldn't want to admit it to others. Not to the neighbors because they wouldn't understand it.

Carl: You can give him credit for being a step better than a neighbor.

Mom: Yes.

(*laughter*)

Dor: Maybe a half step.

Carl: A half step? Sorry.
   So what else happened during the sessions?

Mom: There were crying sessions. Vanessa was dramat-ic during one.

Mar: There were pillows to punch with.

Mike: And Gail wouldn't do it.

Mom: Dad and I fought. No, it was just me. He wouldn't fight. Just like Gail.

Carl: So he's to blame.

Van: Mom had a lot of tears. Dad talked about feeling

defeated and cried. There
was a sense of your life being
over. I remember I was glad
to be there when you were
feeling so bad.

Dad: Yes. I figured I'd never
accomplish what I did. It got
me to toe the mark and get it
done. Time runs out if you
don't get going. Like I figure
that Marie is nine years
younger than me. If it goes
according to age, she's got
nine more years to suffer than
I do.

(*laughter*)

Again, a touching gesture
from a man who isn't accus-
tomed to the world of words.

Carl: What was it in the
interviews that made you
flip?

Dad: Well, it was pointed out
that I wasn't . . . you kids
were always around Mother
and I could never be around.
I never was close. I figured
the only thing I could give to
all of you is the house. Now
you have a house to come to.

Van: I appreciate it.

Gail: I've seen Mom and Dad's
relationship really flourish. I
see them a lot. Dad has tried

hard. Mom's adjustment has
been harder because she's
more isolated. She needs to
reach out and branch out to
others like I do.

With the tone so upbeat, the very real difference was increasingly apparent. I wanted to directly inquire about this shift of
attitude. I wanted to hear how the rest of the family now viewed
and related to Dad.

Carl: I had the feeling last
time, I'm not sure how
accurately I remember it,
that the family was in general
angry at Dad. Is that true?

All: Yes!

Carl: Has that changed? I had
the feeling that Mother was
angry at Dad. It feels now
that she still feels badly about
his not being more intimate
or personal with her, but it
feels like there's more lovingness in the way she says it
now.

Van: I can say how it is for
me. I was more angry at you,
Dad, three or four years ago
for the various things you did
or did not do. Now I feel
more accepting of you. I still
don't . . . I'm aware of not
feeling real close to you, but

it's not the anger. More the
distance.

Carl: Now you'd like to be
close, but you haven't made
it. Before you didn't want to.

Van: Yes.

Another change is clear. Now
Vanessa is more able to see
her father as a person, not
just a role. She can sense
wanting a relationship with
him, not just wanting to
escape the tyranny.

Gail: I'm closer to my parents
now. I had some subtle anger
at Dad before, but not now.

As the session began to near an end, I made one more open-
ended offer to hear more about how the family had changed.
Vanessa decided to take the opportunity.

Carl: So what else?

Van: I think the family sessions
have brought us closer as a
family. I can see it with Mom
and Dad. Especially since you
moved into that house. It's
like your relationship is on a
second start.

Mom: Yes. Well, with no kids,
it helps.

Mom takes the opportunity to
share a basic change in her
perspective. She implies that
with the kids gone, she and
John may decide to develop
their relationship. There's
even a hint of enjoying it.

Perhaps she's over being a nobody.

Van: I think it helped me with relationships. The kind of people I'm choosing now are very different. I feel the sessions helped in that way.

Carl: I had the feeling that one of the things I've noticed being different is that you seem more serious. Before, I had the feeling you were kind of laughing at yourself.

Van: Yes. I feel more serious.

Carl: More willing to put your guts into it.

This is one of the real goals of therapy. To free people so they can get their guts involved in living. To really experience life, not just think about it.

As the session closed, there was a sense of relaxation and calm. They were not panicked about the prospect of being left alone with each other. There was no sense that they needed me to have the courage to be them. They had formed a family set and I was clearly more on the outside than previously.

Their expanded sense of freedom and courage was striking. They openly discussed their capacity to enjoy, not just tolerate, being with each other. They had developed the capacity to really be with each other. To look at life and to respond in a truly caring, personal manner.

As the therapy ends, it also continues. The family carries the therapist with them and the therapist has the family inside. As life goes on, the therapist is left with the excitement of having been involved in a touching human experience.

REFERENCES

Betz, B., & Whitehorn, J. C. *Effective Psychotherapy with the Schizophrenic Patient*. New York: Aronson, 1975.

Bowen, M. *Family Therapy in Clinical Practice*. New York: Aronson, 1978.

Camus, A. *The Myth of Sisyphus*. New York: Random House, 1955.

Kaiser, H. In L. Fierman (Ed.), *Effective Psychotherapy: The Contributions of Helmuth Kaiser*. New York: Free Press, 1965.

Kopp, S. *If You Meet the Buddha on the Road, Kill Him*. Palo Alto, Calif.: Science and Behavior Books, Inc., 1972.

Minuchin, S. *Families and Family Therapy*. Cambridge, Mass.: Harvard University Press, 1974.

Winnicott, D. Hate in the countertransference. *International Journal of Psychoanalysis*, 1949, 30, 69–79.